Help For The Tempted

And That Means All of Us

By

Amos R. Wells

"More Than Conquerors"

First Fruits Press
Wilmore, Kentucky
c2015

Help for the tempted, and that means all of us, by Amos R. Wells.

First Fruits Press, ©2015
Previously published: Boston and Chicago: United Society of Christian Endeavor, ©1903.

ISBN: 9781621714033 (print), 9781621714040 (digital)

Digital version at http://place.asburyseminary.edu/christianendeavorbooks/24/

First Fruits Press is a digital imprint of the Asbury Theological Seminary, B.L. Fisher Library. Asbury Theological Seminary is the legal owner of the material previously published by the Pentecostal Publishing Co. and reserves the right to release new editions of this material as well as new material produced by Asbury Theological Seminary. Its publications are available for noncommercial and educational uses, such as research, teaching and private study. First Fruits Press has licensed the digital version of this work under the Creative Commons Attribution Noncommercial 3.0 United States License. To view a copy of this license, visit http://creativecommons.org/licenses/by-nc/3.0/us/.

For all other uses, contact:

First Fruits Press
B.L. Fisher Library
Asbury Theological Seminary
204 N. Lexington Ave.
Wilmore, KY 40390
http://place.asburyseminary.edu/firstfruits

Wells, Amos R. (Amos Russel), 1862-1933.
   Help for the tempted, and that means all of us / by Amos R. Wells.
   182 pages ; 21 cm.
   Wilmore, Ky. : First Fruits Press, ©2015.
   Includes index.
   Reprint. Previously published: Boston : United Society of Christian Endeavor, ©1903.
   ISBN: 9781621714033 (pbk.)
   1. Christian life. 2. Temptation – Biblical teaching. I. Title.
BV4501 .W455 2015

Cover design by Jonathan Ramsay

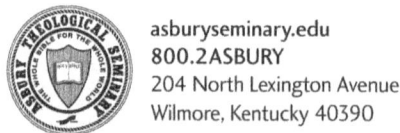

asburyseminary.edu
800.2ASBURY
204 North Lexington Avenue
Wilmore, Kentucky 40390

First Fruits Press
The Academic Open Press of Asbury Theological Seminary
204 N. Lexington Ave., Wilmore, KY 40390
859-858-2236
first.fruits@asburyseminary.edu
asbury.to/firstfruits

HELP FOR THE TEMPTED

Help For The Tempted

And That Means All of Us

By AMOS R. WELLS

"More than Conquerors"

UNITED SOCIETY OF CHRISTIAN ENDEAVOR

BOSTON, MASS.

Copyrighted, 1902, 1903,
By AMOS R. WELLS.

Copyrighted in Great Britain.

Contents

		PAGE
	A Word with You	7
I.	Help from Confidence	9
II.	Help from a Mastered Mind	16
III.	Help from a Full Mind	25
IV.	Help from Christ's Presence	34
V.	Help from the Thought of Eternity	43
VI.	Help from Mortification	51
VII.	Help from Widened Interests	60
VIII.	Help from a Vigorous Body	68
IX.	Help from Hell	76
X.	Help from Heaven	84
XI.	Help from Human Dignity	93
XII.	Help from Vigilance	101
XIII.	Help from the Atonement	110
XIV.	Help from the Bible	120
XV.	Help from Prayer	129
XVI.	Help from Out-of-Doors	138
XVII.	Help from Recreation	147
XVIII.	Help from Confession	155
XIX.	Help from Conscience	165
XX.	Help from Friendship	174

A Word with You

HAVE written this book to help myself. It has helped me, already in the writing of it, and so I hope it will help you.

For the world is so full of sin! Whoever you are, though I know nothing else about you, I know that you are a sinner, as I am; tempted, as I am; struggling, as I struggle, against fearful odds.

Never dare call yourself a less sinner than another man—or a greater. God alone sees men's hearts. Compared with God's purity all men are equal in sin, as both lily and coal are silhouettes against the sun.

Yes, the world is so full of sin! How many are the letters I have received, I, an utter stranger, from the antipodes and close at home, from plough-boys and ministers of the gospel, confessing the most beastly sins, desperately and pathetically reaching out in the dark after sympathy and help! This book is my answer to such letters.

And my answer also, as I said, to my own need, or it could not hope to be an answer to the need of any of my brothers.

For the world is full of help. God has not left any man alone with Satan, nor with only one weapon against the devil.

I have found all these helps helpful, one at one time, one at another. I cannot arrange them in order, for no man's temptations are orderly; temptations are essentially disorder. And though not all by any means help me equally, I cannot arrange them in degrees.

Whatever helpfulness this book has, therefore, will not be discovered by a single reading. It is to be kept by you, carried with you, reviewed again and again, loaned to our brothers in sin and temptation, copies of it given away, and read in the light of their lives as well as our own. This book has taken fifteen years to write; it might well require fifteen years to read.

May the Father, whose loving Presence has been very close to me while I have been writing these pages; may the Holy Spirit, whose recognized guidance has led me into whatever truth they contain and preserved me from whatever falsehood they do not express; and may Christ, my Friend, my Brother, my Saviour, my Helper revered with all adoration, help me and help you, as the blessed God is so eager to help, out of every weakness, sin, and snare, and into the strong humility, the obedient, glad purity, of the sons of God. Amen.

Help for the Tempted

I

Help from Confidence

THERE is only one unconquerable sin, and that is the sin you are not trying to conquer.

If you loathe your sin, though at the same time you love it, there is hope for you, and as long as you loathe it.

For the sin—never forget this—is not in the deed, but in the mind; and while your mind hates the deed and tries to flee from it, do not dare to think yourself wholly lost.

Do not dare, I say, since thus you discredit the power of the Almighty, whose impulsion is beating in your conscience.

Men sometimes ask me, with horror and disgust, whether they have committed the unpardonable sin. Always I must say, " No, my brother, so long as you fear it and are ashamed."

They have committed the unpardonable sin who sin until they reject pardon, spit upon it, make a mock of it, and forget that they have sinned. Every sinner is speeding toward that awful hardness, but he has not reached it while he can bemoan his iniquity.

Be of good hope, then, though daily for years you have fallen into the filth you despise. Sin is a foul stream, but it is a narrow one, and the firm bank is ever near. Ever near—until you reach the black ocean.

And you have not reached the ocean while you can see the river-bank, and long toward it with a great outreaching.

Let your conscience be your confidence. Dark it is around you, how dark! but while that bell rings you are not utterly lost.

Remember: you are not to think about your hold on God,—feeble, inconstant,—but about God's hold on you.

Remember: you are not to reckon up your failures, but dwell on His successes. How often He has conquered sin!

Remember: you are not to consider each fall—alas, so many!—as a fall still farther from Him; for He is in every

Confidence   11

place, no nearer the highest archangel than the lowest sinner.

Though ten thousand times, after sinning, you have sworn, "That shall be the last," swear it after the ten thousand and first.

"It is ten thousand times less likely to be the last than the first sin was"? Yes, yes, ah, yes, if you look at your poor, weakened, miserable self. But Christ has not grown weak with your ten thousand sins. And He is your Reliance.

"But I am ten thousand times less likely to turn from my sin to Him than I was at first." True; sadly true; but *He is there*, and as close to you as at first; and you have only to turn.

Oh, rouse in you the unconquerable will! Do not for a moment acquiesce in defeat! Do not for a moment say of your sin, "It has become myself!" Hold it aloof in your clinched hands. Have no expectation but of the day when you will be free from it.

Nay, assert your instant freedom from it. Do not postpone your emancipation. Let Now be your day of salvation. It may be Never, unless it is Now. And it can be Now.

Men conquer in battle by their confidence that they will conquer. Napoleon's assurance wrought as much as

Napoleon's armies. Much more may you be confident, for instead of an arm of flesh you may have the Everlasting Arms.

Despair is reliance upon self. You have proved it a broken reed. "I will not," you have said; and your next heart-beat has pulsed after your sin. "I will not," you have said, and even while saying it have known that you would.

But hope is reliance upon God. With Him, to desire is to will and to will is to do.

Say to yourself: "Though I fail again, as I have so often failed, it will not be God failing."

Nay, do not say, "Though I fail." Do not admit the possibility of failure. Say to yourself, "I cannot fail, now. It is God, now, and no longer I."

You are cheating yourself if you say, "It is God, now"? In your heart you know, "It is sin, still"? Well, is it not glorious to be so cheated? Will it ever be true unless you believe it true?

Brother, take Christ at His word! "Though your sins be as scarlet, they shall be white as snow." "Ask, and ye shall receive." "Thy faith *hath* saved thee; go in peace."

Confidence

Whosoever is saved from his sins must be saved in his sins. A drowning man may not pull himself from the sea and then be saved.

Whosoever is saved, about him at one moment beat the black surges of his sins, overwhelming, horrible, not to be overcome; and beneath him at the next moment lift the Everlasting Arms.

Your despair is now no greater than it will be just before you are saved. You will not be saved by your confidence, but by Christ,—His hands stretched out in pity to yours flung up in impotence.

Learn what it means, "When I am weak, then am I strong." Gather confidence thus from your impotence. No lack in all the universe but there is a supply. The deeper the pit, the readier are the waters to fill it. And how deep is the pit of your despair!

If Christ were in Sirius, well might you faint; but your Confidence is by your side.

If Christ were ever at a loss, well might you faint; but your Confidence is Omnipotence.

If Christ ever turned away, well might you faint; but always it is men that turn away from Christ.

Then be confident in Christ, brother! Dare to say, "I am saved!" Not "I hope I am saved," but "I *am* saved!" Not, "I hope I shall be saved," but "I *am* saved!" Dare to assert, "I am done with sin, for I have begun with Christ." Clothe yourself in His armor, and know yourself invincible. Do not dream of defeat; dream of Him. Do not look to yourself; look at Him. Do not remember the past; remember Him who has become your stainless and inevitable Future.

And daily, hourly, pray this prayer:—

Lord Jesus, with a boldness of peace I trust in Thee. Thou hast never failed a soul that trusted in Thee, and Thou wilt not begin, even with my wretched soul. My sin is no longer mine; it is Thine; O Infinite Condescension, it is Thine! Thou hast borne it away from me, far as the east is from the west. I am clean, and I will forget that foulness. I am strong, and the memory of my weakness shall pass away. When to-day the tempter comes, I shall be with Thee. When to-day the old allurements call, I shall listen to Thee. When to-day my heart sinks down in anguish of horrible longing, Thou wilt be my defense against myself, and Thou wilt become my desire. I have no fear, for Thou art my assurance. Not even do I fear

Confidence

myself, for Thou hast become my Self. No more sin, O Thou my Purity! No more shame, O Thou my Honor! No more wavering and despair, O Thou the Immutable Christ! To Thy love be the glory, time without end. Amen.

II

Help from a Mastered Mind

NO one is tempted from without, but from within. It is not circumstances that tempt you, but desire; not matter, but mind.

The lily draws purity from the slime, because itself is pure. The sensualist, into his rotten heart, would draw impurity from a lily.

One of the easy tricks of the devil is to persuade you that not you, but fate, is responsible for your sin; not you, but things and happenings. *That is, God;* but God tempts no man. Neither does the devil tempt any man from without. It is not necessary, and the devil wastes no work.

No; when you are tempted you are drawn away of your own lust and enticed. Manfully stand up to that.

And so the conquest of temptation is not the conquest of things, but of thought.

I am asked, "Where *shall* I go, to be free from this sin that is eating out my life?" Nowhither. What avails to

A Mastered Mind

transplant a tree while the worm is at the heart of it?

I am asked, "What shall I *do?* Into what sea of business shall I plunge, and escape my sin?" Work is healing, but it is not the knife. A cancer is not to be cured by sawing wood.

Look within. Sternly put away your cowardly excuses. Sternly acknowledge that no chance for sin would be a chance without your choice. Sternly say, "I—I—I—am the sin. God help me!"

The sinner's task is to master his mind. Here, in a few pounds of flesh, intricately folded, lies your battle-field of the brain, a battle-field some seven hundred square inches in area! Conquer here, and you shall conquer everywhere else. Play the craven here, and demons shall mock you to the pit.

For is it not laughable that man, who can clean great cities and carry water over a continent, cannot clean these little gutters of the brain? Is it not absurd that man, who can raze forests and cast mountains into the sea, cannot erase a desire from his mind?

"Mister" means "master," and "mistress" means "masteress"; but many a "Mr." and "Mrs." would more truthfully write themselves down "Mastered." Mastered John Doe! The slave of a desire!

I am learning, when temptation comes, to make my mind ice to it, so that it can get no foothold; stupid to it, so that it can grasp no interest; blind to it, so that it can only fumble in the dark; numb to it, so that the thrill of its pleasure is blunted; dead to it.

I cannot well describe the sensation. It is almost as if, at the approach of temptation, I were to take my brain, so curiously folded upon itself, so full of dark furrows for sin to lurk, and shake it swiftly, desperately out, till all its folds are smooth, their contents gone, the mind a safe and happy blank.

And so I hold myself, oblivious, tense, withdrawn, until the stress of temptation is over, until I have summoned to my aid the heavenly powers.

It is like a moment's trance, into which I fly for safety, as a knight of old would put on his helmet of invisibility. And while I am asleep, the danger often passes.

It is as when a babe falls into mischief, and the nurse, by a sharp and disconnected outcry, so distracts the baby mind that when she is through, he forgets what he was about.

This timely dulness and vacancy of brain serves me better on a sudden assault of temptation than an active defense, as a barricade of cotton is more effective than a barricade of bricks. So the shrewd Japanese practise a deadly gymnastics whereby their bodies become fluid before the rush of an antagonist, who dislocates his shoulder or breaks his neck by sheer force of his own unopposed onset.

But there are many ways of mastering the mind, as there are diversities of mind to master. You may not make another's way yours, but you must make yours the spirit of mastery, the genius of self-control.

For what avails it to have the power of swift thought, the godlike skill of transporting your spirit instantly from America to Persia, from this modern moment to the building of the pyramids, if that power is to whirl you shrieking away whither you would not go?

An automobile, a "self-moved," is a wonderful machine so long as it is *not* self-moved, but glides smoothly, intelligently, at the twist of its driver's hand. But it is a terrible machine when it runs away.

Oh, assert dominion over yourself! Raise on that mighty continent the banner of authority! Let it be no empty banner, like Maximilian's in Mexico, but heavy with determination, and its spiked pole thrust deep into the soil!

Be not half your own, and that the surface half, while the inward realities are in base subjection. The white ants of Africa eat out the inside of boards, leaving an unbroken exterior shell, so that an entire table will seem solid, yet crumble at a touch. Be not such a man.

Convert your nature, by whatever furnace fires and workshop hammerings, into tempered steel,—facile, yet solid; keen, yet strong; swift, yet enduring. Move as one. Be not divided against yourself. Become a whole.

Make your mind an obedient tool. What if the carpenter's hammer should get on occasion a handle of flexible rubber? What if his chisel should wear when it chose an edge of putty? What if his saw should fly out of his hand and set itself to sawing the piano leg? His tools would be no greater outlaws than many minds.

You *cannot* control your feelings? You *cannot* guide your emotions? You *cannot* master your mind? You do what you would not, and what you would not you do? That is to be, in those points, insane!

Why! suppose your tongue, when you bade it say "horse," should say "acorn"; or your legs, when you wished to go forward, should turn backward; or your hands, when you desired to open a book, should throw it out of the window. Would you not be alarmed about yourself? And will you view with equanimity a parallel condition of mind?

What! you can shut your mouth or open it when you choose, clinch your fingers or stretch them out, close your eyes or admit the light; and has God so formed you that your *mind* must be always open, for the access and free use of whatever foul emotion or sinful passion chooses to enter? Has God made you master of all parts of your being except the part most necessary for you to master, the controlling part, your feelings?

Never say that you cannot help your feelings, that you *must* be gloomy, or lustful, or passionate, or intemperate, or heedless; you were made that way. That is to slander your Maker. You were NOT made that way.

No; you were made to move as an ordered universe, your Will at the centre as absolute lord. You were made to say to this emotion, Come, and it will come; and to that feeling, Go, and it will go. God never fashioned you to be slave of that most ignoble serfdom into which you have fallen, that bondage to your own base appetites.

"But I am in that bondage," you cry, as myriads cry in their anguish. "I am lost in that serfdom. How can I ever get out? How can I ever find my sceptre and my throne?"

Brother, there is no mastery for the finite except as it is mastered by the Infinite. Sooner could you grasp the reins of the stars, sooner could you guide the galaxies along their way, than hold the leash of your passions—alone.

You have tried it, and you know I am right. By a thousand failures you know it. By humiliations without number, by self-abasements beyond count, by grovelings of the spirit and a frenzy of impotent grief. And you could go on thus forever, with your unaided will, groping wildly after the mastery of your mind, and grope in vain.

Only by submission to the Spirit of God can you control your own spirit.

Is it not so in all other matters? Can you make a house stand firm except as you yield to God's law of gravitation? Can you sharpen or consolidate a sword but by obedience to God's law of heat and cold? Can you move an engine save through serving God's law of expansion? Long ago men learned in the material world to expect no mastery but through point-by-point subservience to the God of nature. Yet we seek without God to govern our souls!

Oh, yield to God, and your passions will yield to you! Get the mind of Christ, and that will master your mind! His very soul is spread before you in His recorded words. Saturate yourself with them. Breathe them in. Drink deep and steady draughts of them. Learn to think in terms of them. Dream of Christ. Talk with Him as you enter the day. Make withdrawal rooms in every task to talk with Him. Efface yourself. Assume Him. Become nothing. Make Him your All.

As you do this, in sincerity, in humility, in steady faithfulness, a power undreamed-of will come to your will. Passions that have lorded it over you will crouch at your feet. Delighted, you will find yourself in control of the chariot of life. Upon its shining axles flash obedient wheels. Fruitful valley and soaring mountain top are open to your range. Out of your flabby, contemptible servitude you have passed into an existence electric with exultant force. Men are moved by you, now. Tasks get easily done, now. There is growth, now, and progress and accomplishment and expectation. You are master of all things, since Christ has become Master of you.

Pray then, brother, pray with wholeness of heart:—

Blessed Saviour, save me to Thyself! I am folly and powerlessness. I am failure and shame. I bring Thee only emptiness and decay. I have no confidence but Thy grace, no merit but Thy mercy. I do not know how even to submit myself to Thee. I cannot loose myself from my chains to fall at Thy feet. I have known sin so long that I do not know Thee, and loved it so long that I do not love Thee, and served it so long that I do not know how to begin to serve Thee. Be Thou my Beginning! Set Thy love where mine should be, Thy perfect service where mine should be, Thy full sacrifice where mine should be, and do for me these things which I only dimly see I should do for myself. I have no will save to have no will. I have so debauched myself that I cannot open the door to Thee. I can only call to Thee. Force it open, Lord! Enter, and rule. Drive out the demons. Let in the fresh air and the sunshine. Take control of my life. I yield Thee the mastery, with full purpose of soul, unreservedly, and forever. Amen.

III

Help from a Full Mind

T is in vacant lots that the weeds grow. To parody the proverb, "Satan finds some mischief still for idle—minds—to do."

Moths do not destroy the garments that are in use, nor do sins corrupt a busy life. It is when the body is relaxed that malaria seizes upon it, and it is in its hour of ease that the soul becomes diseased.

An army is broken by the gap in its front, a fort is taken by the unoccupied point of the wall, and it is through the vacancies of the brain that devils enter.

I find it healthful to have no unclaimed minute for the fiends to claim. By preempting all the territory of my time I keep out evil immigrants.

I find so many arrows flying abroad that I live my life under cover, and this continuous roof I place over my head is an ordered, comprehensive plan.

Let those that are sorely tempted by any sin heed the injunction, "*Oc-*

cupy—till I come!" Occupy! Fill up the space! It is to the empty house, swept and garnished, that the devils come.

Mortgage your day to God before it begins. Form a plan for every instant of it. Live by schedule. It is the stagnant stream that rots. Keep your mind moving.

Especially, where your temptation most easily and often assails you, there crowd in this barrier of occupation, as the dyke is made thickest opposite the strongest surges.

Is it when your opening senses are half aroused by the dawn of a new day, and your vigor is relaxed by slumber? Do temptations master you then? Let an alarm-clock startle you into entire wakefulness. Leap from your couch with no debate. Seize on your dumb-bells or Indian clubs. Put your body through its paces and cause it to remember subjection to your will.

Is it at some special season during the day that sin gains easiest control, as when you meet this person or that, when you must pass a certain place, see certain sights or hear certain sounds? Contrive for that time your most urgent business. It is the swift runner that is not swerved from his course.

Is it as you lie down at night, worn by the day, that demons press in among your distractions and readily subdue you to their will? Then cultivate an overmastering weariness. With fierce toil of brain and body, and especially of the body, so exercise yourself that from every nerve and muscle and from every corner of your brain will come the cry for sleep. Though you must toil till midnight, continue till the passion for slumber has crowded out all other passions.

It is good always to have a book at hand, a book you will read because you enjoy it. Save the small books to carry with you wherever you go. Keep a pile of books by your bedside. In the cars, on the street, at your work or your play, be companied by a good book.

Often it will benefit you when you are not reading it, by the very pressure of it in your garments reminding you that it is there, as the presence of a friend is helpful though he may say no word.

There are few defenses against temptation like the studious habit. It does not so much matter what truth you study as that you study. It is undisciplined minds, like undisciplined troops, that Satan's cohorts drive before them.

A will that sets itself day after day to tread the path of English history is little likely to stray into the by-paths of debauchery. A determination that mounts with strenuous delight the rugged heights of mathematics will not grow flaccid under pressure of temptation. The steady purpose that masters geology or German through the plodding of uncounted days and the careful economy of time will not easily be mastered by iniquity.

In times of peace the soldier must go through all the motions of war, or, at the first onset of the foe, we shall have no soldier. He must load and fire daily, though only blank cartridges; he must fix bayonets, though only to charge into the empty air; he must fight, though only in sham battles. Obedience to orders must become a habit, courage and firmness must become instinctive, heroism must be drilled into a commonplace and an inevitable.

And so it is in the armory of some studious toil that the soul trains itself for the conflict with sin. The fibres of the mind grow sturdy, the powers of the mind become facile, swift, and imperious, as they wrestle with facts, and conquer some domain of science.

Novel-reading and newspaper-reading will not bring this about, any more than a soldier could be made by leap-frog and tag. Leap-frog and tag are well in their way, but their way is the meadow-path, and not the highway over which armies march.

Yet do not think to conquer temptation without recreation. The camp-songs do as much for the army as the military band, and the camp-jokes as the exhortations in the orders.

No room is fully occupied that is occupied with cannon-balls. There will be many nooks for something lighter to fill.

No day is well planned that does not plan for play. There are two charms that send the foul fiend packing; one is the Lord's Prayer, and the other is an honest, hearty laugh.

Only, *play* when you play. Give yourself wholly to your happiness. *Occupy* your sport, make it an occupation, here also leave no gap in your interest through which the devil may flash.

And a great help, in this struggle with temptation, is an avocation, a "fad," a side employment. In your house, whatever space is not filled by the furniture should be filled with pure air; and your avocation may become the pure air of your life.

It may be binding books, as Gough did, and thus undoubtedly he triumphed over many an assault of his great temptation. It may be filing newspaper clippings—my own especial joy! It may be flowers or fiddle, butterflies or beetles, painting or poetry, fancy cakes or flying-machines. Whatever it is, so it be innocent, it will blessedly fill the crannies of your day, and help you to occupy—till He come.

But these are artifices,—games and hobbies, and such indirections. They are devices that must be used, for many an end useful and refreshing. But the full mind will depend on no health outside itself, just as the prudent mind dares not.

For amusements and avocations are the sport of circumstances; and a rainy day, or sudden business, or a sickness of you or some other, may throw your prop into the middle of next week. Lean not hard on such a staff; especially in this imperative journey, this flight from sin.

A full mind! Better than a full dwelling, though packed with the spoil of exquisite travel. Better than a full library, though levant and morocco make fragrant half a mile. Better than a full pocket, though weighed down with diamonds. Better than a full drawing-room, though crammed with earth's wisest and loveliest.

For a full mind is a palace, crowded with all delights and utilities. It is a library, whose books can be read in the dark. It is a fortune that no panic can shake. It fills your life with friends immutable by distance, differings, or death.

A full mind! that is fuller the more you take from it; always inviting, always rewarding, always more fascinating than any allurement of vice. There is no medicine like this. This is the true gold cure for the drunkard. This is the golden cure for all drunken passions whatsoever.

And how to get it? Not by flabby wishes. Not by haphazard effort, careless outreach. Not thus are even houses filled, nor even pockets. Not thus, surely, is an immortal mind filled with eternal properties.

No; but thus: "Whatsoever things are true, whatsoever things are honorable, whatsoever things are just, whatsoever things are pure, whatsoever things are lovely, whatsoever things are of good report; if there be any virtue, and if there be any praise, THINK ON THESE THINGS."

"Whatsoever"—the widest range, the deepest research, the fullest comprehension. Not a snatch here and a fragment there. The entire domain of truth, purity, and loveliness.

"Think"—not the pedant's cold collection, that fancies he owns a truth because he has labelled it and pigeonholed it, but that warm, loving, persistent brooding over a truth that alone absorbs it into your soul.

And "on THESE things," and no others. Surely the field is wide enough. All art. All literature. All philosophy. All history and biography. All science. All philanthropy. All religion. I have named eight vast continents. Ah, when your mind, my brother, is at leisure from your necessary toil, is there a single one of these eight to which it hastens, eager and fleet as a schoolboy to the playground? Is there one of the eight where it feels at home, where it has made even a beginning of ownership?

Oh, when we think how empty our minds are, how wretched companions for themselves, how little we know of God and His world, and to what trivialities and bestialities we turn at a moment's leisure, we need not wonder that our minds fall easy prey to foulness, worry, anger, covetousness, and all other iniquities.

a Full Mind

So let us pray, and having prayed and as we pray let us act:—

¶ Infinite Creator, Revered Maker of all these wonders of the world, these marvels of the mind, Thou hast spread before me a full table, and I have been eating husks with swine. Thou hast called me to the throne room, and I have lived in the cellar. Thou hast offered me diamonds, and I have filled my hands with dirt. And when I have deserved punishment, to be choked with the offal or blinded in the cellar, Thou hast continued Thy proffer and Thy pleading. Forgive me, Thou Holy and Gracious! Even yet admit me into Thy fulness! Even yet lay hold upon my interests, and convert them to Thyself! Wean me from the love of folly to the love of worth. Rebuke my sloth, and transform it into energy. Rebuke my heedlessness, and change it to ambition. Sternly drive out the demons, and occupy, oh, occupy the mansion of my soul! Amen.

IV

Help from Christ's Presence

YOU do not know Christ, or you do not know His presence with you, or you would not sin.

Many a man has sinned in Christ's presence, but he has not known Him. Many a man has known Him, yet sinned, losing sight of Him and forgetting Him.

To know Christ it is not enough to know about Him; the devils know about Him, and tremble. The knowledge of Christ that saves from sin is not thought out but lived out; it is not a conclusion but a conquest; it is not an understanding but an undertaking; it is not an appreciation of Christ's character but an apprehension of it: That is why many a man who thinks he knows Christ, yet, to his dismayed perplexity, continues in his sins.

And to know Christ's presence with you, it is not enough to know that He is present. John knew it, yet slept in Gethsemane. Peter knew it, yet denied his Lord.

Christ's Presence

The knowledge of Christ's presence that saves from sin is no vision of the eyes or understanding of the mind. For days a man sees a woman, but on one holy day he realizes that he loves her; then for the first time he knows her presence. Shall the knowledge of Christ's presence be less than that?

I think that Christ's entire life in the flesh was only to teach a very few men to see Him present in the spirit. But the joy of such a vision must be passed on, and through those few men will yet come the saving of the world.

Has the vision come to you? Is your thought of Christ yet more than a thought? Is it a Person?

Is Christ, in your honest view of Him, a Galilean carpenter lying dead in Syrian soil? When you picture Him to your fancy, is your picture in the past tense? Do you imagine Him as He was, stilling the tempest on Gennesaret, and not as He is, quieting the storms in human souls?

When you think of Christ's words, "Blessed are the pure in heart, for they shall see God," do you hear the words as an echo from the grassy slopes of Hattin, or as a warning and a promise spoken out of the living ether, in tones as vivid as your wife's or your mother's, to the immediate, personal hearing of your heart?

Not as the mesmerized see unsubstantial visions, not as a dismantled brain is peopled with fretful ghosts, but as in walking down street you accost Friend Hazen, and as to your parlor you admit Mrs. Rader, so clearly and certainly do you walk with Christ?

When your eyes first open from the mystery of sleep, does Christ, in no poetical fancy but in the most definite fact, bend over your bed, His breath warm upon your cheek, His eyes looking love into yours, and purity, and power for the day? Do you say to Him, "Thank you for life again, dear Christ; and what shall I do with it to-day?" Do you say it aloud, to Him hearing it and replying?

Do you go to your day's work with Him? I do not mean in any mystical sense, as you would go with Patience, or Prudence, or Courage, but as you would set out with your brother to cut a tree-trunk, he at one end and you at the other of a cross-cut saw? as prosaically, as surely, as gloriously?

When happiness comes to you in the day, do you turn, the first thing, to show it to Him? When you are perplexed or saddened or dismayed, do you lean back upon His shoulder and whisper

Christ's Presence

to Him awhile? Is there no helper among the creatures of flesh so personal, so masterful, so indubitable, as He?

Does He sit beside you at the desk? Does He bend beside you over the counter or the stove? Does He swing with you the tennis racquet or the golf stick? Do these suggestions appear fanciful to you, half profane, or do they seem the merest every-day occurrences? Would it be His *absence* from these common scenes that would be unreal to you, unbelievable, terribly strange?

Ah, my brother, work must be done; yet it will be well with you if you say, "I will set about no task to-day until Christ goes with me." The world is beautiful, enjoyable; but it will be well with you if you say, "I will take no pleasure to-day until Christ takes it with me." That is never a task for you, or a sport, to which you must go Alone. Better stop where you are, and for days wrestle with your evil heart till it is overcome, if you *can* go anywhere Alone.

Would your thought of Christ's presence become more real to you if you could touch Him? if He would take in fleshly hand your hand of flesh? if His speech vibrated upon the veritable air, and you could photograph His face? Would all this render His presence a whit more real? Then you do not yet know His presence as real at all.

Do not cheat yourself with vain imaginings, with opinions dressed up as a Person and philosophy masquerading as a Fact. There is no midway between personality and impersonality. Either Christ is to you a Person, and so all that I have pictured, or He is only a world-memory, a sentence in a book, an idea in the brain, a thing.

And Christ cannot be to you a person without being *the* Person,—test your faith by that fact. If He is real to you at all, He is the Supreme Reality; wiser than your father, more loving than your mother, dearer than your wife, more engrossing than your children.

And thus, O tempted soul, when you know Christ's presence, you will, you must, cease from iniquity. Think of that sin! Would you commit it in the presence of father or mother, wife or child? How much less in the presence of One dearer, more loving, than all!

It is easy to confuse your judgment, to trick and cozen your conscience; but you know that you cannot cheat Him.

It is easy to forget your good resolutions, but you cannot forget Him, looking at you.

It is easy, there by yourself, to postpone honor, and purity, and self-respect, and manliness, and think you will be

Christ's Presence

stronger next time; but you cannot postpone Him, speaking to you.

And you will not want to cheat Him, forget Him, put Him off. Truly perceiving Him, His love, His beauty, His might, you will have no wish but to do His will. The shadows will melt into His light. The uncleanness will be swallowed up of His purity.

How shall we come to realize this Presence, how may we live with the Lord? Not without toil and striving; not without continuance of purpose; not without paying the price.

The price is but an asking, but it is a great asking. It is the asking of desire, a hunger that longs irresistibly after Christ, and will not be wheedled with half-christs. It is the asking of meditation, long hours fixed upon the one theme, to get at the heart of Christ, which lies at the heart of the Book. It is the asking of surrender, the abandonment of hindrances, the loathing of carnal lusts, the mortification of the body, the repression of the world.

No double asking, reaching with one hand after Christ and with the other detaining sin, will draw Christ a hair's breadth nearer. No half-asking, fitful, aimless, hopeless, will win the Beautiful Presence. It must be the asking of your entire soul, and its only asking.

Do you wish to be alone? Would you pollute sweet solitude with your sin? Then the thought of Christ's presence is displeasing to you.

Do you still, while you fear your sin, longingly anticipate the scenes and comrades of debauch? Then you will not long for Christ's companionship.

While you clasp the darkness, you will never come into the presence of the light.

And until you experience it, you must believe the report of its joy. You must listen to rescued sinners who cry to you out of its joy. You must grope toward it blindly, with what heart you can. You must believe, and ask Christ to help your unbelief.

Your life, I say, must become an asking. Only by prayer, varied and persevering prayer, is the Presence to be won.

As you enter the night, whose holy silences are compelled to hide shudderingly so many foul deeds, pray for the Presence. As you enter the day, which may become a star in your crown or a brand in your burning, pray for the Presence. As times or places or moods and occasions of temptation draw near, pray for the Presence. As you walk along the street, passing entrances to the pit, pray for the Presence. As you ap-

Christ's Presence   41

proach an hour of leisure, when your mind is free to work its evil will, pray for the Presence. Nay, at all seasons and in all chances, since it is when no one expects him that the devil comes, pray for the Presence.

Somewhat thus, however disjointedly and stammeringly, so only your soul be in it, as an undertone through your day and when you awake in the night, pray for the Presence:—

Lord Jesus, who canst save me because Thou wert tempted in all points as I am, yet without sin, come, come, come to me! I dare not live without Thee. I am trying to live without Thee. The spirit of evil within me persuades me ever away from Thee. The law of sin and death holds sway over me. But with what of my heart I own, I cry to Thee, Come, come, come! Pity my helplessness, and come. While Thy justice condemns me, the forger of my own chains, yet come, come! Be kinder than my blinded prayers, be truer than my half-sincere entreaties, be more swift, oh, more swift than my temptations, and come, come, come! Take this prayer, this fragment of will and righteous desire, and bless it and increase it as Thou didst bless and magnify the bit of bread. Help me to hate my sin, now. Help me to be a man, now. Help me to remember how brief is sinful pleasure, how long is pain. Show me Thyself, in Thy compelling glory. Bear my need as a prayer, and come, come, come! In Thy name, Lord Jesus. Amen.

V

Help from the Thought of Eternity

WHAT is the issue of life? Eternity. What is the object of life? To make character for eternity. What is the reward or punishment of life? Character—for eternity.

Do you ever dare think of yourself? Of what do you think, at that time? Of your body—such a form and height, such a complexion, eyes and hair of such a color, garments such and such? Of your attainments—so much Greek and mathematics, so much skill in carpentry or pie-making or law-making? Of your possessions—this house and that, yonder bookcase, your gold watch, your diamond brooch, your bonds and mortgages? Do you think of these accidents, these bubbles that momently shine around yourself, or do you think of that self as it is?

As it is, solemn, mysterious, momentous. As it is, enduring while the earth endures, and more; while the sun endures, and more; while the universe and all universes endure, and more; while God endures. As it is, the one significance among these shadows, the one substance among these shows.

Is eternity a name to you; or is it, and your portentous union with it, the apex of your dreaming, the throbbing undertone of all your hours?

For eternity is a chain, every link a century, which you may pay out till it girdles this great globe, and repeat it as many times as the globe has grains of dust, and you will scarcely have begun eternity. Your eternity.

And eternity is a thought, stretching out as far as thought can reach, over countless abysms of time, and met by a relay of another thought, and that again by another, and another, and another, till the thoughts are as many as the stars in the sky; and still not all of them will have made more than an entrance into eternity. Your eternity.

And eternity is a snail, setting forth to crawl to Sirius, measuring a year with every length of its slow body, and returning thus from Sirius, and repeating the stupendous journey as many times as there are snails in the world, and yet not measuring a single span of eternity's infinite reach. Your eternity.

And eternity is an acorn, which becomes an oak, which bears a million acorns, and each becomes an oak, to bear acorns each of them and those to produce oaks, till all space has become a forest, and every singing leaf on every tree bears record of a different century, yet all together do not sum up an hour of eternity. Your eternity.

So that the longest pain, the heaviest weight of woe, the most appalling difficulties with which your life could be filled on earth, are lighter, more flitting, than a butterfly's wing, compared with the unimagined horror of a sad eternity.

So that the maddest merriment, the keenest pleasure, with which a long life on earth could be packed, is only a baby's gurgle of laughter, compared with the sparkling, sunny reaches of a blissful eternity.

And if it is true, or if there is only a chance of its being true, that character here formed is formed forever, that some shall go away into this everlasting life and some into this everlasting death, what question overtops this question, what interest or what mass of interests matches this, what business, of all our myriad employments, is not baby's finger-play beside the making of character?

And it is true. By every law of nature, definitely ordered, endlessly moving when once set in motion, you may know it true. By every observation of men, growing hardened in their sins and with each year less easily reclaimable, you may know it true. By every struggle with your sin, which rests the heavier upon you each day it is endured; by every exertion of your conscience, weaker and weaker with each defeat, you may know it true. By the words of inspiration, which tell us that now, while our hearts are not finally hardened, now is the day of salvation,—you may know it true. By the words of our divine Lord, who came out of that eternity to testify of it to us, whose lips, so willingly attuned to love and mercy, yet foretold a time when He must say, " Depart, ye cursed, into everlasting fire,"—by His explicit, repeated teachings we may know it true, that character, here formed, is formed forever.

Take heed lest you rebel against God's love and infinite wisdom. Take heed lest you complain, and think this life too short for results so vast, so endlessly momentous. Are you not glad that your eye is so delicate that a single slip of the knife may blind you for a lifetime? And would you have your soul less delicate? Are you not glad that you can fix your character in virtue, that you can anticipate a time when you need no longer watch your impulses, bridle your desires, fight your sins; and can you imagine the possibility of virtue-fixation without the possibility of vice-fixation? And have you any reason to think that a double trial or a quadruple would change the result? Is not God, who made the infant, best judge of how long the infant shall be forming its body into manhood, and shall He not best determine the maturity of the soul?

Be sure that infinite mercy will shine through infinite justice. Be sure that no feeblest desire for the good will ever be quenched of God. Be sure that no sorrow will rest upon a single soul that He can withhold. Be sure that all our decisions are made by ourselves, down to the final decision, hurried in no instant by God, darkened in no point by His anger, no allowance being refused that can be granted, and no opportunity being denied that can avail. Be sure that God, who knows all the stretch of the future, can tell at this instant what you will make of yourself,—can tell it as thoroughly as if He had waited many eons. And be sure that He will permit you to make of yourself what you will.

Would you have it otherwise? Would you have the Infinite Hands lay hold of you, wrench you away from evil, clamp you forcibly to virtue, fasten you to a derrick and swing you into heaven like a log of wood or a piece of stone? Then you would cease to be a man, you would become wood and stone, and all the significance of soul would have gone from you.

Do not rebel at the thought of eternal torture. Our Father tortures no man. The torture of hell is self-conceived, self-inflicted. Would you prefer the annihilation of the wicked? Do not allow your fancies to play with such a theme. It is not for human preference to toss the issues of eternity. Only be sure that the eternity is our Father's, and that even hell will be ordered as is best.

But oh, brother, brother, dare you think of eternity? Can you face that endless prospect undismayed? Whither are you tending? Are you sure? Fearfully sure or blessedly sure?

When next you are tempted to sin, think of the endless life. Nay, think of it before the temptation is on, that your will may be tense and your heart armed against it.

What is a moment's gratification of an appetite, matched with the endless years? What is the stress of the combat, though you labor nigh to death fighting against sin, when you think of the prize before you? Will you be insane? Will you be infantile? Will you barter eternity for a mouthful of sugared arsenic?

Thought of Eternity

It is easy, after sinning, in remorse and fear to think these thoughts. But the victory lies in thinking them at sin's approach. Safety lies in weaving them with the substance of your mind so that they become instinctive, so that you live no longer under the power of sin, but in the power of the endless years.

You cannot do this without meditation upon eternity, long communion with the thought, guided by the Bible, which is eternity's Handbook.

Refer everything to the standard of eternity. Ask of this pleasure, "Is its joy a part of the eternal joy?" Ask of this labor, "Is it a task that can be continued in a happy eternity?" Ask of these words, "Are they consonant with the language of heaven?" Ask of those thoughts and emotions, "Would I have them repeated endlessly through the ages?"

And whatever is doubtful under this test, though it were a hand, cut it off, and though it were an eye, pluck it out. That is no maiming which moves you toward a happy eternity, that is no loss which turns the scale by a hair's breadth toward eternal happiness.

And do not think to effect an iota of this by yourself. Only the eternal Christ can win eternity for you. Only the Conqueror of time can tear you from the moment's debauch into the ceaseless joy. Only the Everliving can set your feet in the way of life.

So to the Eternal Christ, who was in the beginning and ever will be, lift daily and hourly this petition:—

Everlasting, Ancient of Days, Thou Alpha and Omega, Thou ceaselessly young and strong and beautiful, save me, oh, save me into the eternal life! Quicken my conscience, buttress my will, that I may tear out the grappling hooks of death, and rise into the eternal life! Be with my thoughts, rebuke corruption in them, confirm what is imperishable, and fix them on eternal life! Be with my ambitions, annul the transitory and trivial, direct the foreseeing, the enduring, and conduct them toward eternal life! Be with this very moment, come to my aid against temptation, pour through my veins the courage of endless years, make this moment Thine, a part of eternal life! I praise Thee for the gift of immortality. Oh, render me worthy of it! Wrap me in Thy worth as a garment, and place its crown upon my head. Not because I merit it, or am in any way other than undeserving of it, but because it is the merit of Jesus and His loving desire for me, I ask it in His blessed name. Amen.

VI

Help from Mortification

MANY things must die, that other things may live. The lower must decrease, that the higher may increase. Ground that is rank with sunflowers will not bear roses. Souls that are absorbed in the carnal will never exult in the spiritual.

The denial of eternal life is never apparent denial; it is the engrossing acceptance of something else.

Of something else, whatever it may be, evil, or only lesser good. It may be some passion of the pit, it may be some selfish-exalted study,—though lust is near to hell and good books are near to heaven, they equally keep one from God if they are chosen in place of Him.

For ours is a jealous God. We bless Thee, our Father, that Thou art a jealous God. Thou art not complacent toward Thy children's undoing. Thou wilt have nothing but their best and happiest.

Our lives are like stairways to heaven, and some stop on the lowest steps, and some are proud that they stop on the highest, but there is only misery for those that stop at all.

God knows this. Therefore He bids us mortify—put to death—our lower nature, crucify the flesh, keep the body under, wrestle with and throttle, as in a life-and-death struggle, whatever prevents our full surrender to Him.

This mortification of our lower nature, this putting it to death, is the sinner's bold assault of temptation, without waiting for it to assail him.

What possession of the spirit is more precious than a will inflexibly righteous? Through all thickets of iniquity it cleaves its way, it parts all barriers of temptation, it turns to rout the most determined onset of evil. When you sin, it is not because sin is strong, but because your will is weak.

What task, then, is better worth achieving than to strengthen your will? What labor, what self-denial, what patience and persistence, are not well spent for such a prize?

For days the athlete will deny his desires, eat what he little likes, drink what is poorly pleasing, agonize in strenuous toil, solely to enlarge and harden a few inches of muscle, and cut a few seconds from a record. The scholar will

Mortification 53

outlast the night with his studies, and twenty years of nights, and wear his body into the grave, all that a new beetle may be named. The worldly ambitious will scant their slumber to the uttermost, scorn the least amusement, place themselves upon the rack of popular debate and hug the rack, lavish long decades in relentless pursuit—of what? Of a name written on a banner, and raised where the winds will tear it to tatters in a month. The miser will starve himself for one more hoarding, the lover will fight fire and wave and tempest for his love, the mother will spend herself, to her last drop of blood and quiver of nerve, for her baby. The world is full of mortifyings, of puttings to death, denying the less or what is thought the less, for the greater or what is deemed the greater.

And when the goal is the greatest and best, your will, your character, your eternal destiny, the happiness of those you love, the welfare of the world so far as you can bless it,—when all this is at stake, when this your all is at stake, how determined should be your striving, how stern your self-denial, how exultant your sacrifices!

But no; alas, no! For an hour's riot, for a moment's thrill, for a pulse of passion, for a whiff of excitement, for a bubble blown of poison, we sell our souls!

Brother, there is no need to paint this madness. You know it. With all bitterness and horror you deplore it. But the madness has fixed itself upon you and you cannot shake it off. You are a madman.

Yes, a madman. When the frenzy of evil is on, it sweeps over your being like the hot simoon, it shrivels your holiest ideals, it mocks your firmest resolutions, it lays bare to passion your very heart. You curse it, you weep, you pray, or think you pray,—and you seek it yet again. Wretched man that you are, bound to that body of death!

Control the frenzy of evil? As readily grasp the lightning! Mortify your passions when they are aroused? As readily put to death the spectre of the plague, when it stalks over the land!

No. The plague is to be conquered before it comes to being. Passions are to be prevented and not controlled. The body is to be crucified before it gets a spirit—your spirit.

Satan's stronghold is in what is not wrong. It is in our subservience to things that " do not matter." It is in our failure to practise mastership in non-essentials.

If your horse is always allowed to have his will when he ambles, he will have

Mortification 55

his will when he runs away. If your rifle is rusty in the barracks, it will be rusty on the sudden call to arms. If you play carelessly in your practice, you will fail in the concert.

Gladstone was observed one day setting out for a ten-mile walk in a heavy storm, and was asked the reason. "Solely because," answered the great man, "I had formed the intention to walk before the storm came up, and I must maintain the habit of carrying out my intentions."

Nothing is trivial that bears relation to the will. It is in small matters that it must be trained, for the stress of great affairs leaves no time for training. If it is not exercised upon what does not tempt, it will falter and fail before temptation.

Be not hasty to form resolutions, but when they are formed, be inflexible. It is of little consequence whether you write that letter or sit idle for half an hour; but that you form the habit of mastering sloth is of infinite consequence. It is of little consequence whether you eat one piece of cake more than you should, or drink an unnecessary glass of soda-water; but unless you are temperate in trifles you will never be temperate at all.

Cultivate decisiveness. In ordering lunch at a restaurant, make quick choice and hold to your choice. In selecting your garments for the day, do not tediously balance this and that, rejecting, accepting, and then returning to what you have rejected. Better make a few mistakes in trifles than make the great mistake of weakness.

If you never deny yourself when it does not count, you will never deny yourself when it does count. You have a horse, and drive him constantly over the right road; now he will find it even in the stormy midnight. You have a will, and accustom it by pleasant daylight to a way; your will will then travel it instinctively when the black storm of passion has torn the reins from your hands.

Keep the body under. Grind your carnal appetites even with undeserved scorn beneath your heel. With fierceness, with a passion equal to their own, force upon them the habit of servitude. Either you or they must rule. Leave no doubt which it is.

Leave no doubt, for the passions are crafty. Under the cloak of submission they carry still heavier chains for you. "See how strong you are!" they cry. "See how well you control us! You are tormenting yourself needlessly. You have proved that you can indulge moderately with safety. See how close

Mortification

you can come to sin, and not actually transgress. For your hand is steady, your will is firm."

Perceive in these suggestions the very horns of the evil one. Meet them with some energy of mortification, some rush of self-denial. When the foul-minded Roman king would reduce his son to his own level of vileness, he bound him and exposed him thus to the temptation of a harlot. The prince bit off his own tongue and spat it in her face. Does this horrible story over-illustrate the fury with which we must repel every solicitation of uncleanness?

We have discarded the follies of asceticism; for asceticism, contrived to conquer passion, became itself a lust and an intemperance. But let us not discard the virtues and power of asceticism, the life of discipline, of endurance, and of conquest.

Learn to live simply. Where a fort is to be defended, they cut away the trees. Often our lives are so ensconced in luxuries that Satan's levies can creep among the foliage unperceived, nearer and nearer, until they surprise the garrison of the soul.

Learn to do without. It is no virtue to fast, but it is a prudence. Be very jealous of your spiritual sovereignty. If you but dimly suspect that this practice or that pleasure is undermining the supremacy of your will, try issues with it at once. Banish it, and keep it in exile till your authority is assured.

And count it no hardship when you thus break with inclination. Feel rather the stern delight of the warrior as he sleeps upon the ground.

For decades William Taylor, heroic missionary bishop, carried with him a stone in a satchel, and at night he used it for his pillow. Some such stone you must get for your living, and you must lie on it as Jacob lay on that at Bethel, until like Jacob you can set it up as memorial of the opened heavens.

All this is easy to say, but oh, so hard to do! *You* cannot do it. Christ alone can do it, in you. Only through the power of the cross can you crucify the flesh. Only through the nail-pierced hands and feet can you mortify your members. Only by grace of Him who rose on high can you keep the body under.

To Him, then, to the Victor, the Victory-bringer, address your continual prayer:—

Saviour, holy Saviour, there is no way of self-denial that Thou hast not walked. Thou didst give up, not one thing, but all things. Thou didst perfectly subdue the

Mortification

flesh. Thou dost know the Gethsemane agony of it, but still Thou dost invite me to Thy path. Trusting in Thee for strength, I enter it, Lord Jesus! I will seek first Thy kingdom and Thy righteousness. I will set my affections on things above. My meat and drink shall be to do Thy will. If my eye is darkness, I will pluck it out. If my hand is iniquity, I will cut it off. I will forget that all good things shall be added to the seekers for Thy kingdom. I will seek it for the kingdom's sake, and the king's. All things shall be loss to me, for the glory of Thy name. What is a world of pleasure, beside Thy briefest smile? What is my will for a lifetime, beside eternity with Thee? What cross, though one by one my desires were stretched upon it, but is an ungrudged ascent to Thee, Thou crucified Light and Life? With all or without all, be Thou my All=in=all, forever. Amen.

VII

Help from Widened Interests

BROAD view of life has come to signify a sane view of it. The Christian is to walk in a narrow way, but that narrow way is to lead into all the world. He is to come out from the evil and be separate from it, and yet he is to be all things to all men.

It is in the lanes and alleys that you find the refuse, while the highways are carefully swept; and so it is among the crowded interests of men that you will lose your soul's impurities, and will meet fewer temptations.

It is never good for a man to withdraw into solitude unless he is sure that God goes thither with him. It is in the wilderness that God Himself was tempted, being in the form of a man. Crowds bring a thousand distractions from virtue, but also a thousand distractions from sin.

And those that dally with temptation make even in the midst of crowds a solitude for their souls. For where the interest is withdrawn from the clean pursuits of men, and fixed, self-centred, upon some wickedness, there is solitude and there is a wilderness, though the man fight daily in the clamor of a stock-exchange, or march in the midst of an army.

Sin is so near akin to selfishness that one is always close to sin when his soul is much alone, and always happily distant from sin when his soul is worthily at work for others. Permit yourself only so much study of yourself as to recognize the truth of this. Perceive, O tempted soul, that the tempting fiend is bashful. Two is company with him, and three is a crowd, when the third is any honest toiler.

Many temptations, to be sure, come in crowds,—such as the revelry of drunkenness, when one plays the fool because another has just played it. But even these temptations are born of solitary brooding, of gloating in secret over the fallacious joys of debauchery; and if even a debauchee will wisely use the time when his fellow-fools are not with him, he will play the fool with them no longer.

Whittier, whose illustrious life was crystal testimony to his words, once told a young man that the way to success lies in attaching one's self in youth to some great, unpopular cause, and growing up into victory with it.

Such also is the road to purity,—attach yourself to some great, pure, absorbing interest.

This interest may well be the cause of human freedom; for many, still, are the slaves. Slaves of rum, slaves of lust, slaves of greed, slaves of ambition, slaves of vanity, slaves of fashion, slaves of poverty, slaves of ignorance, slaves of superstition, slaves of pride! Join with the preacher, the missionary, the reformer, the teacher, the philanthropist!

Let not these great names appall you. No one is rightly living his life—no one, man, woman, or child—unless he is, so far as he has power to be, a preacher, a missionary, a reformer, a teacher, and a philanthropist!

Unless, so far as in you lies, you, Christian, are teaching the truth of God at home and abroad, and correcting what is evil and furthering what is good,—what do ye more than others?

The worldling is a man of the centre; the Christian is a man of the circumference. At that centre lurks the spider, sin.

Widen your interests, my brother, if you would flee the devil. I do not mean a diffused life; concentrate all you please, but concentrate upon the large concerns of the Kingdom.

Widened Interests

Consider the healthfulness that flows from the single interest of missions,—the outlook over all the world, the insight into men and customs, the acquaintance with history, the knowledge of exalted biography, the development of the practical and the ideal, the enlargement of sympathies, the deepening of brotherhood, the increase of generosity, the verification of faith, the sense of comradeship with God!

In proportion as this great, clean interest, so multiform, so manly, so fascinating, takes possession of a life, its uncleannesses are driven out. What room is there for them any longer? It is a fresh, sweet broom of many fibres, sweeping the hidden corners of the soul.

Who can consort daily with Henry Martyn and be licentious? with Allen Gardiner and be a drunkard? with Paton and be a miser? with Livingstone and be an egotist? with Patteson and be a glutton?

Who can feel the woes of the women of India, the oppressed of Turkey, the slave of Africa, the priest-bound of Peru, the superstition-fettered Chinese, the miseries of poverty, ignorance, and heathenism in our own land, and not take shame to spend on his lusts a cent of money or a pulse of power?

I am needed for the world! This is a truth that will cleanse me and keep me clean. I am needed, every coin, every minute, every thought, every shred of talent, every atom of strength!

No one is taking my place; few are taking their own. No one, though all the world besides were at this work, *could* take my place.

Such a feeling of responsibility for others purifies like the outward-rushing fire. The feeling is to be gained from other work than missions. The temperance reform will give it; so will civic reforms; so will work with young people in Sunday school and young people's society; so will labor for the poor; so will toil for the sick; so will prison ministries; so will city missions; so will the activities of King's Daughters, Lend-a-Hand Clubs, Brotherhoods of Andrew and Philip, and a thousand other Christly fraternities.

But remember, the healing is from within, not from without. It is not in what the hand does, though it sign a dozen constitutions, carry flowers to the sick, carry good reading to the prisons, carry food to the poor. It is in what the mind does.

When men wish to cleanse a swamp, they have but one problem: to get the water to running out. So when you

Widened Interests 65

would purify your mind, there is only one problem : to set its interests to flowing outward.

They may turn the swamp down hill by under drainage; they may turn a hill upon the swamp by pouring a river in; they may lift the swamp into the clouds by cutting down the tree-barriers that shut out the sun. There are many ways of cleaning a swamp, and a mind; but they all tend outward, they all transform the swamp from centre-life to circumference-life.

Do not say that you are incapable of large interests, of widened thinking, that yours is a little mind. The smallest swamp may breed as poisonous malaria as the largest one; but also, the smallest stream may become a part of the greatest river. I am not urging you to greatness, but that you ally yourself with it.

And yet there is no surer way for even a small mind to become great than by concerning itself with great interests, and there is no surer way for even a great mind to become small than by attaching itself to pettiness.

Begin—anywhere and any way! Take up some book on missions, on philanthropy, on reform, on any aggressive Christian work, read it, and it will be your guide to other books and those to others. Do something to help others,—

something, anything; that deed will be your guide to something else you can do, and that to something else. Find some one who is an outgoing Christian, —some one, any one, an individual or a society, and do something in that companionship; it will open up other associations, till you are in touch with the army, and feel the thrill of countless elbows.

I have not spoken about the mental widening that comes from a delightful study, such as some line of history, science, language, or literature, or some charming pursuit, such as photography, or some enriching amusement, such as chess or tennis. I have felt that the swamp is very deep and foul, and that these streams, running level with time, are rather weak to cleanse it. I would turn into the swamp the impetuous currents of the eternal hills.

Live in the greatest things you know! Soon you will cease to know the belittling things.

Be proud to make the humblest beginning of a great matter rather than the most complacent achievement of a trifling one.

Stride abroad with Jehovah! At first you must toddle like a babe at His side, but He will soon get you to walking like a man.

Widened Interests

And so make this your true petition to your Father in heaven:—

Maker and Controller of all things, take me out with Thee into Thy vast horizons! Ransom me from this prison, whose walls are creeping ever in upon me. Show me the sweep of Thy providences, the majesty of Thy scope. Redeem me from self-love. Enrich me with self-sacrifice. Fire me with holy ambition. Set my feet in a large room. ¶ I will no longer dwarf my soul with sin. ¶ I will reach forth to manly thoughts and manly tasks. ¶ I will reverse the currents of my interests. ¶ I will seek others' gratification, others' welfare. ¶ In lowly imitation of my Father, in proud and happy imitation of Him, ¶ I also will become interested in all things, and helpful. It will be because Thou dost dwell in me, Lover of all! And it will be in Christ's name and for His sake. Amen.

VIII

Help from a Vigorous Body

HERE are some things that the devil hates worse than good health, but not many things.

If you have constant headaches, toothaches, backaches, eyeaches, if you are always morbidly tired and never happily tired, if your digestion goes wrong and your circulation is poor and your liver out of order, Satan has a holiday so far as you are concerned. Why tempt a man who carries a battery of temptations around with him?

There have been saints in spite of wretched bodies, saints like Henry Martyn, Robert Hall, Elizabeth Browning; but it was in spite of their bodies, and in sore despite.

It is often said that avoidable sickness is a sin. It is a sin, and the herald of twenty more.

Watch yourself and your sins. Do you not most often fall when your physical stamina has fallen first?

A Vigorous Body

Every muscle, when it is not flabby, is a stout barrier against sin. Every nerve, when it is steady, is a steel network behind which you are safe. Every organ, when it is not in rebellion, is a trooper on guard against iniquity.

But when the brain is fagged out and the body anæmic, when the heart beats weariedly and the lungs are clogged, when the stomach groans at its impossible task and the nerves and muscles lie inert and despairing, then bestial temptations come mockingly in, altogether unopposed.

What resolution can be upheld by a body so near to unholy dissolution? What spiritual grace can be maintained by those that disgrace their physical natures? Who can fight Satan and dyspepsia at the same time? Surely none but a spiritual giant.

You have struggled against sin long enough to know how fierce is the combat, how feeble are your resources at the best, how desperately you need them to be at their best. Where all are sorely inadequate,—body, mind, soul,—do you not see what folly it is to permit one to relax?

"But is not God my Helper?" you may ask. "Is He not Spirit, and omnipotent? Can He need my wretched body for a weapon or a tool? Has He not bidden me *not* to trust in an arm of flesh?"

Ah, brother, God's Word declares that of this omnipotent Spirit the very temple is—man's body. Not only the temple, but the workshop, the arsenal, the fort. You are to trust no arm of flesh, but you are to trust God's arm—*in* an arm of flesh.

Does not the very word, *super*natural, presuppose the natural? Will you remove the natural from under the *super*natural? Why, the church, Christians, you and I, make up the body of Christ, the only body He now has on earth. It is through our eyes He must see; shall we not keep them clear? through our muscles He must work; shall we not preserve them strong?

Revere your body. Revere it as God's handiwork, the marvelous climax of creation, since not in the melodious mazes of the universe is there a harmony so wondrously attuned as here. Revere it as God's abiding-place, His church where all other churches fail.

Revere it in deeds, not sentiment alone. Warm it—with good food. Ventilate it—with fresh air. Cleanse it—with hearty exercise. Treat it at least as well as a church of brick and mortar.

a Vigorous Body

Temptations assail you, brother? Knock them down with dumb-bells or Indian clubs! Run away from them on the bicycle—they can never keep up! Nay, walk away from them, and if you foot it briskly, over hill and dale, you will find the club-footed fiend a poor pedestrian!

Or rather, do not wait till temptations assail you. Provide a vigorous body against their coming. They will see its glittering towers from afar, and slink back into their dens.

Is a bit of ground open to your tillage? Learn what virtue dwells in a lawn-mower, a hoe, a rake, a spade, a wheelbarrow! You'll keep your soul clean, I'll warrant, if you get your hands thus dirty!

Do you or can you own a work-bench and a box of tools? Discover how much of Jesus' victory in His temptations sprung from the sturdy carpenter life that preceded!

Let it not be aimless toil, whatever you do (though health is aim enough), for interest flags without a concrete goal. On your bicycle—go somewhere. With your Indian clubs—swing toward a definite arm-girth. On your plot of ground —raise a crop. With your tools—furnish the house.

It is good never to go to bed until you can lay there a tired body. Often you think your body is tired when you are only worried, and your brain-tire would vanish if your body could be tired. Bring it about, though you must go out and race for two miles in the dark.

A tired body, so tired that slumber comes quickly, irresistibly, dreamlessly, is a glorious ally of purity and power. Such sleep is the best of exorcisms against the devil.

Some will need to be warned against becoming too tired, overwearied, so that they cannot sleep. That is also the devil's chance. *Any* excess is his chance.

But of those that are continually tempted to sin and as continually fall, by far the greater part lead flabby lives. Their physical stamina is down at the heel, and so is their spiritual stamina. Their gait is languid, and so is their Christian "walk." Their bearing is slouched, nor do their souls bear themselves uprightly.

Not only do men set their teeth and clinch their fists when they are determined; set teeth and clinched hands *make* them more determined. Not only do men lift their heads and straighten their shoulders when they are alert and hopeful, but a brisk bearing renders them more alert and hopeful, as any one may prove if he will.

I do not believe that even the Bread of Life can nourish a soul while the body in which the soul lives is fed with fried potatoes, strong tea, mince-pie, and brandy.

I do not believe that any spirit can sleep the sleep of the just while the accompanying body is paying the penalty of insomnia for dietetic sins.

I do not believe that any man can be strong in the Lord and in the power of His might while he is deliberately or carelessly weakening his body.

I do not believe that any one can lay up many treasures in heaven while he is squandering on earth the God-given treasure of health.

I think it likely that many who read these lines may be moved to take a few walks, or buy a pair of dumb-bells, or join a gymnasium, or clean up their bicycles. I think it more than likely that the most of these many will take only three walks, forget their dumb-bells after the third morning, attend the gymnasium only three weeks, and ride their bicycles no more than three miles!

Health is a harvest. It must be worked for. The seeds must be sown, and carefully tended. There must be persistence in the tilling and patience in the waiting and vigor in the gathering.

A stout body must be planned for. It does not come at haphazard,—a game to-day, rowing to-morrow, next week an hour in the garden, then a fit of the home exerciser. You would not make money that way, nor can you make muscle.

Enter upon the work with system and intelligence and purpose. Get some good book on health (and none is better, for sprightly sense, than Blaikie's " How to Get Strong," published by Harper's). Adopt a regimen, chosen after careful experimentation upon yourself. Having adopted it, pursue it, though the heavens fall.

If it is walking, walk, though the devil send a tornado. If it is Indian clubs, swing, though the devil push the thermometer to one hundred. If it is gardening, garden, though the devil hurl at you a thousand mosquitoes.

Do not hold health a secondary matter, subordinate to business, subordinate to pleasure. Business and pleasure are at its mercy in the long run, and so is a higher than either.

Your body is a temple of the Holy Ghost. Return ever to the one great argument. In proportion as you honor the Spirit of the Living God, you will come to honor His living temple.

a Vigorous Body

Build high its walls of health! Let them glisten white with purity! Cement them with firmness of will! Found them on obedience to law! Adorn them with the carvings of enjoyment! Crown them with the pinnacles of a holy ambition!

And ever, in your work for the body, pray thus to the God who formed it:—

Infinite and Holy, for whom the universe is a body, Thine arm the outreach of gravity, Thy feet the light, Thy brain the ether! Bodies innumerable Thou hast created and Thou dost uphold. To man alone Thou hast given charge of a body. Oh, solemn and glorious dignity! I would be worthy of it. I seek Thy mind, to guide me. Thy mind, to which the care of an infinity of bodies is no task, grant me a portion of it, loving Father, for my own heavy task! Help me to clear vision, to steady purpose, to invincible purity. Confirm my righteous will and scatter my temptations. Dwell increasingly within me, and as Thou dwellest, transform. For Jesus' sake. Amen.

IX

Help from Hell

ELP from hell! Is anything but hindrance in that thought? Should I not rather have written, Help from heaven? Yes, that also; but still, Help from hell!

For the fear of the Lord is the beginning of wisdom, though the love of the Lord is its continuance. If we feared hell more, we should sin less. If we loved heaven more, we should the less desert righteousness.

If the thought of heaven were more helpful than the thought of hell, Christ, the great Helper, would have spoken more of heaven than of hell.

What did He, the loving, the merciful, mean when He said, "These shall go away into eternal punishment: but the righteous into eternal life"? He that is our only Testimony to eternity, shall we receive the pleasing half and reject the terrible half? Shall we presume to fancy an eternal heaven and a transient hell? Shall a man, forsooth, be more loving-wise than Christ?

What did He, the gentle, the lowly, mean when He said, " Depart from me, ye cursed, into everlasting fire, prepared for the devil and his angels "? What did He mean by the " wailing and gnashing of teeth," " where their worm dieth not, and the fire is not quenched "? What did He, the Light of the world, mean by " the outer darkness "? What did He, the Saviour of all, mean when He threatened, " Except ye repent, ye shall all likewise perish "? What did He, the meek, the humble, mean when He cried, " Ye serpents, ye generation of vipers, how can ye escape the damnation of hell ? " What did He, who came to reconcile the world to His Father, mean by the " great gulf fixed," and Dives on the other side in " a place of torment," the scribes and Pharisees " thrust out," the wicked " severed from among the just," the sheep to the right and the goats to the left, the fruitless tree, the tares, cut down, gathered, and cast into the fire? What did He mean by all this, and much more?

There are some things He did *not* mean. He did not mean that God sends any soul to hell ; the wicked merely go to their own place. He did not mean that God torments any soul in hell ; the fire of hell is kindled by the wicked and kept alive by their wickedness. He did not mean that God delights in hell ; how

God grieves over it—that grief is the Incarnation!

But there are some things that, with all the infinite truth and love and majesty of His divine nature, He *did* mean by this teaching.

That God has founded His universe upon justice, and will not, *can*not, bless the unrighteous.

That God has established His heaven in consistency, and will not, *can*not, admit to it the unheavenly.

That God is essential good, and to choose God is endless joy. That away from God there is no good, and to reject God is endless woe.

That it is possible to accept God with an eternal acceptance and reject God with an eternal rejection.

Oh, dark and awful certainty of hell! Sure as the radiance of heaven is thy gloom. Sure as the love of Christ are thy torments. Immutable as the permanence of eternal life is eternal death.

Where is the helpfulness of this thought? Shall we not rather run from it, as so many do, and hide our heads from it, though only in the sand? Shall we not deny it, though at the cost of denying Christ?

Hell

It is helpful as the danger sign is helpful, warning us away from bog, or thin ice, or pestilential house. It is helpful as bitter herbs, that also are medicinal. It is helpful as a lightning flash, that shows at our feet a precipice.

For God wills that all men everywhere should repent. Could God have His way, still permitting us to be men, hell would to-day be empty, and every soul of the dead be happy in His heaven. The revelation of hell is a revelation of God's anxiety for His children, a revelation not of God's hatred, but His love.

Oh, what wretches then we are, knowing all this, still cleaving to our sin! Oh, what fools we are, seeing all this, ever shutting our eyes against it! Oh, what madmen we are, hearing the warnings, yet choosing the way of death!

Let us say no longer, with silly, complacent doubt, "*If* there be a hell." Let us no longer, in fatuous security, refuse to consider hell. Let us no longer, as the hypocrites do, think of the wicked there, but of ourselves as good.

It is well to meditate on hell. Not in gloom and morbidness, not in fearful despair, but with clear eyes and steady heart to look, if we are Christ's, at the pit whence we have been dug; and if we are not Christ's but are yet in our sins, that we may realize, before it is too late, whither those sins are hurling us.

To be "without," "in the outer darkness," "severed," and forever! To look across the great gulf, and see beyond it the lights of home, from which we are eternal exiles. To see our dear ones there. To see there the loving, serving, glorious Christ. To see blessed companionship there. To see all loveliness there. To catch the last wave of their songs, the final hint of their fragrance. And to know around one's self only blackness and loneliness and death. And after all not to care, but with a torment of passion to love darkness rather than light, and death rather than life, forever! That is hell.

Were there only a possibility of it, instead of the truth it is, would it not be worth the toil of a lifetime to escape it and help others to escape it?

Be a man, be a man, be a man! That is no place for you. It was not prepared for you, but for the devil and his angels.

Be a man, be a man, be a man! Resist the devil, and he will flee from you. You will not be tempted above what you are able to resist.

Be a man, be a man, be a man! Bid Satan behind you. Have done with

Hell

him and his. Be your own master, and a slave no longer.

"Alas," you cry, " I have tried to be a man, but I am no man. I have longed for mastery, but my serfdom settles the heavier upon me. I have commanded the devil behind me, but he will not stay there. I have resisted him, but he keeps coming back again."

Why not, since even after our Lord's victory in His temptation, the devil left Him only "for a season"? Shall the servant be above his Lord?

Fight on, and look for no end of the conflict on earth! Drive the devil away, but ever watch and pray against his renewed attacks. Fight on, ceaselessly, victoriously,—as you may, if you do not fight alone.

For there is One—never forget it—who has conquered hell; One, and only One. No man ever conquered it, but the God-man. Now, with Him all men may conquer it.

Alas for you if you realize hell but do not realize Christ! That is to see the chasm but not the bridge, the plague but not the physician, the enemy but not the reinforcement, threatening death but not victorious life.

Standing by the side of Christ, His hand upon your shoulder, you can look without a tremor upon the great gulf, you can face the great enemy without a fear.

Christ knows your despair, your myriad failures, your increasing powerlessness. To His might it is all one whether you have failed a thousand times or only once. "Let not your heart be troubled," He says, " neither let it be afraid."

Christ is adequate to any emergency. No sudden rush of temptation can surprise Him, no heaping of demonic allurements can seduce Him, no exhibition of satanic power can daunt Him, no weakness or defeat of yours can discourage Him.

Oh, hell is deep, but Christ is taller than hell! Temptation is a giant, but Christ's finger is stronger! Sin is a poison in all our veins, but Christ is Health, regnant and everlasting!

Therefore will we not fear, though the earth be removed. Christ is in the midst of us, and we shall not be moved. He is our Refuge and Strength, a very present Help.

O my Saviour, Lord of heaven, art Thou not also the Master of hell? I bless Thee for Thy plain words of terrible warning. I bless Thee for the promises interwoven with the threats. I glory in Thy stern=

Hell

ness as in Thy love. ¶ too would see things as they are, sin in all its hideousness, penalty in all its woe, that I may also see Thee in all Thy might of helpfulness. Make as clear to me Thy hell as Thy heaven. Grant me Thy conquest over the one, Thy inheritance of the other. ¶ take glad refuge in Thee. ¶ shall henceforth forget my fears, remembering Thee; forget my shame, remembering Thee. And I shall take courage even from my failures, since they force me ever nearer the Unfailing One. Amen.

X

Help from Heaven

IT is the present-day fashion to urge men to do well in the hope of business advancement, a fat bank account, power in a corporation or a vast trust, a fine house, and the envious honor among men which these rewards produce. It is not the modern fashion to hold out as a life-incentive the hope of heaven. We are seeking a heaven on earth.

But heaven is not on earth, though the kingdom of heaven, its fundamental principle, is. Nay, that kingdom, that claim, certainty, and authority of heaven, is within every heaven-directed heart.

The kingdom of heaven that is on the earth, in the hearts of believers, is only a distant, island colony of heaven itself. As the United States is only faintly mirrored in the Philippines or Great Britain in the Falklands, so heaven is but dimly seen in its earthly outposts.

No one can prepare himself for the next world by confining his thought to this world; as well prepare yourself for a visit to those queerly named " Ce-

Heaven

lestials" in Asia, by cooking to-day's breakfast or ploughing your corn-field, with no glance at geography, guide-book, or sailing-list.

No one can live well in this world unless he fixes his affections on things above this world, and beyond. If the ploughman would plough straight, he must not look at his feet in the furrow, but at the other side of the field. If the surveyor would avoid confusion, he must refer all lines to the North Star.

The devil works through the lower appetites. He does not know how to tempt a man who is hungry for heaven. He is at home in fishing for you, but is at a loss when you fly.

Most prudent is it therefore for the tempted man that, though his body must remain for a time in the devil's sphere, he lift his mind and interests above it, to the heaven where no sin enters, and no temptation to sin.

O my brother, beset by passions, bond-slave of your sensual desires, break the bonds, stamp the world beneath your feet, live in the home of the soul!

How unreal is heaven to you! How unreal it must be, not to draw you, with invincible soft compulsion, from the slime! Is it not, to your apprehension, a place of ghosts, of inane occupations, of empty, bloodless, unsubstantial living? Do you not think of heaven as floating somewhere among the clouds, as filmy and faint as they? No wonder such a heaven cannot draw you from your lusts!

Brother! heaven is more solid than anything on earth! When John wrote out his vision he was led to picture it in terms of the most compact substances known to him,—gold, glass, jaspar, precious stones!

See how God loves the material world, —grass, trees, rocks, beautiful flesh, beautiful form,—even as He has taught you to love it. See how He exults in new fashions of it, and lavishes upon it the outpourings of His evident interest. Is all this for our whiff of time? Is it not rather only a foretaste of eternity? Will the Creator be different in heaven, and may we not know His likings there from His likings here?

But God is a spirit, you say, and a spirit has no flesh and bones, nor is a spiritual world a material one.

Not material like this world, let us gladly believe, with its volcanic crust, its dying trees, its fading flowers, its wrinkled flesh, its deafened ears and age-dimmed eyes! Not perishable matter, but, of whatever matter, solid and substantial!

Heaven

For consider what makes substance; is it not your realization of it? Would the ground seem substantial to you if you could sink through it, as a spirit can? Would that door seem substantial to you if you could pass through its mass, as Christ could? May not God have created a spiritual world that is as solid to our spiritual apprehension as this material world to our fleshly touch? And when we enter our spiritual bodies, will it not then be this world of matter that will seem unreal and ghostly?

Banish, then, your fancies of a misty heaven! They are unscriptural, unphilosophical, absurd, born of nurses' tales.

Fill heaven with real things, with books that can be handled, with flowers that can be plucked, with trees that can be climbed, with houses whose floors ring to the tread! Do not stop to remind yourself that these actual things cannot be there; what corresponds to them will be there, as real, as familiar, as comforting.

People heaven with real folks, children that can be hugged and kissed, men with whom you can shake hands, flesh that is firm to the touch, color that comes and goes in the cheek. Do not stop to remind yourself how gross this picture must be. It is spirituality itself compared with the common conception of our spiritual bodies as floating bubbles, with wings.

To tell a child that dolls are in heaven, a music-lover that pianos are there, a book-lover that morocco-bound folios are there, an artist that paint brushes and color tubes are there, is the least of blunders compared with permitting them to form a ghostly idea of heaven, or no idea at all.

Be certain, whatever form heaven takes, that it will be as real as earth. Be certain, whatever new properties and joys will grow upon our knowledge, that heaven will not rudely startle us with strangenesses, but will be a familiar place, a dear place, home. And be certain, in it all, that heaven is infinitely better than the best of earth.

For there will be no death there, and no sin.

No death, but always the bright eye, the bounding step, the blush of health, the exhilaration of power, the delicate fascination of beauty!

No sin, no temptation, but white souls that cannot be stained, pure thoughts that cannot be fouled, heads that can forevermore be held erect!

And so no sorrow there, no shadow of a tear, no shame or memory of shame, no loneliness or fear of loneliness, no anxiety or dread, no more talk, even,— no more thought, even, of the miserable sins we have grown so used to! How strange, how heavenly strange, it all will be!

But work, there, the work we shall like the best, the work we can do the best, unhurried, never fruitless, never unpraised! And play, there, the enjoyment we shall like the best, with the comrades we love the best, unmarred, exultant, and serene! And rest, there, as long as we wish, as long as we need, when and where and as we wish it and need it,—ah, how good it will be!

These are no fairy tales. These are only the plain revelations of Christ, who proved beyond question His knowledge of what He spoke. As certain as gravitation, as certain as the pyramids, as certain as the stone foundation of your house, are all these truths of heaven.

Will you not make them vivid to yourself, so that they may become working factors in your life? Do you not see how powerfully it will aid you in resisting temptation to keep ever before you this substantial blessedness, this solid, unspeakable glory, from which sin will infallibly shut you out forever? Having once seen it, will you give yourself longer to baubles?

Dream, then, of heaven. Read all that revelation tells you of it. Meditate long on each particular, and discover all that it implies. Think often of the persons that must be there. Take them one by one, as you would review the neighbors in your street, for they may be your neighbors on your street in heaven.

Let your fancy play about the theme. I think the Bible tells us so little about heaven, not to rebuke our curiosity, but to pique it, and excite our imaginations, knowing that the happy reality far surpasses imagination.

Plan your mansion there, how you will have the rooms. Will not Christ, who allows you to build your house here, let you have your liking there?

Plan your days there, what you want to do, whom you want to meet, what in all the universe you want to see. You will plan wiser and happier days, the nearer you get to Christ.

Recur often to the thought, as the sorrows and evils of life assail you, "It is not so there." When sickness comes —"It is not so there." When temptations allure—"It is not so there." When iniquity triumphs—"It is not so there."

Do not fear that all this will make you visionary, unpractical. They are the visionaries, they are the unpractical, who

Heaven 91

cheat themselves with baubles, and pursue the mirages of time, neglecting the substance of eternity.

Do not expect heaven to become real to you at once, or without persistent wooing. "It is only heaven that is given away"—yes; but it is given only to long desire, patient determination, the spurning of the unheavenly, the eager and constant gaze beyond.

In all your temptations therefore, and when sin is at a distance preparing an approach, make this your earnest petition:—

Father in heaven, take me to heaven! As it is done in heaven I would do Thy will on earth, that I may come to do it in heaven. Forgive me that I respond so seldom to Thy calls, Thy drawings upward. Forgive me the folly that pulls me down to the beasts. Show me Thyself, who art heaven! Thyself, in whom sin's power is vanquished, vanished. Thyself, the Beautiful, the Desirable. I love Thee, and I would love only Thee. These lower things that I love, and loving hate, and hating despise, oh, drive them out of my life! I will supplant the passions of earth with a passion for heaven. As hotly as I have pursued them I will seek it, and Thee. I will bring to the true standard my sense of realities. Things transient shall be ghostly to me, and the eternal things shall be substantial. Implant within me Thy kingdom of heaven, O God, and bring me safely to my coronation day! Through riches of grace in Christ Jesus my Lord. Amen.

XI

Help from Human Dignity

WHEN next you are tempted to sin, think of what you are, think of your origin, think of your destiny, think of the plans God has for you, think of the possibilities open to you, think of the dear ones dependent upon you, think of the life you might live, unmarred, growing in beauty, growing in power; and hold up this picture of your ideal self as a shield between you and temptation.

We care not when a horse's hoof splashes in the mire; but, alas, when the sandalled foot of a princess falls there!

We take no heed, though a thousand cheap chromos are burned up; but the whole world would mourn at the loss of the Sistine Madonna.

Oh, bethink you, when next you hunger after some pollution, what work of a Master you are about to defile! What harmony in your body you are about to turn into discord, what majesty of mind you are about to lower into filth, what excellence of hope, what proud alliance with eternity, you are trampling beneath your feet!

Know yourself to be a child of God. That will be meaningless unless you know God; but, knowing God, it will be a perpetual crown.

A child of God; for are you not made in His image? Those feet, that slink to dens of foulness; those eyes, that gloat upon vileness; your mouth that swallows iniquity and speaks poison; your brain that hoards debasement like a miser,—how in them all you put to shame the image of God!

A child of God; for have you not received of His nature? Can you not reason?—and persuade yourself to sin! Can you not plan?—and devise schemes of evil! Can you not make choice of good?—and, alas! make choice of unrighteousness.

A child of God; for are you not called to His work? Is it not yours to subdue the world?—and behold, you are subdued by it! Is it not yours to create joy?—and see how you are fashioning sorrow! Is it not yours to live for others?—and your life is turned in upon yourself! Is it not yours to win souls to God?—and alas, alas! your soul is Satan's!

A child of God; for you are to live forever! Evermore to sit with Him as joint owner and ruler of heaven, or sit with Satan in the everlasting gloom of hell!

Hold up your hand—the rarest, most wonderful, most perfect of tools. View your body,—no engine runs so well; your ear, your eye, your tongue—what marvelous faculties of hearing, vision, speech! Consider the casket of your skull, and whether the round earth contains matter more intricately skilled! What leagues of thought lie coiled up there! What seeds of fancy have burst there to forest or jungle! What a continent is folded within a hand-space!

Yours is the Koh-i-noor of God's creation; will you scratch idly with it upon the rock? Yours is the sceptre of time and eternity; will you use it to stir up mud?

Reverence thyself! for there is so much of God in thee. Crush rare porcelain beneath your feet, tear rich garments to tatters, hurl your watch against a boulder, but revere your body and your mind in their least powers and functions, for they are the workmanship of God!

To abuse even your eyes or your teeth with careless usage, to abuse your stomach with foul drink, to abuse with passion those creative powers in which man is nearest God,—all this, in their degrees, is to abuse the God within you, and set at naught the God above you.

Reverence thyself! Not a deed or thought of lust but burns up a thousand prayers. No act or desire of intemperance but crushes some noble ambition.

Reverence thyself! Thy life is a holy cathedral, majestic with lofty arches, lovely with pictured windows, shot through with color, pulsing a noble song. Not a temptation resisted but deepens the radiance of its glory; not a temptation received but darkens the panes, stills the music, and infects the masonry with decay.

What chances you miss, when you fall into sin! Never once has the trap caught you, but the King has passed by!

Now it has been a child to help, and your soul was too full of bitterness to yield comfort. Now it has been a word to speak for God, and shame has held your tongue. Now some door of great usefulness has opened to you, and you, who could not rule yourself, have not dared take direction of others. Not once have you poured out your strength for Satan, but some urgent need has demanded that strength for God.

Human Dignity

Since the world is so full of need. Are there not many that look to you for their cheer, their guidance, their support? Can you ever sin to yourself alone?

Nay, there are threads from your life to all the world! Let sin cut any thread, and something, many things, must go awry.

To be a man, and to do a man's work, requires no atom less than all your time, your powers, and your desire. Every minute spent in sin, every waste of nerve or muscle upon it, and every motion toward it of your mind, assures that you are less a man, and will do less than a man's work.

Has God given you to teach? When temptation next assails you, say, "That, or some new truth; that, or my strength for patience and enlightenment."

Has God given you to write? On the next enticement to sin, say, "This foulness, or some pure poem; this vileness, or some inspiring essay."

Has God given you a home? At the next impulse to iniquity, say, "That, or more money for my wife, more smiles for my children, more honor for the family I have founded."

There is no man living who does not walk attended by a more than royal retinue; well if he has eyes to see it! There are the good and great who have gone before him, in his church, his calling, his village,—all the nobility of character whose examples should speak to his soul. There are his friends, his loved ones, the living who are bound to him so closely. And there are the dear ones who have died, his mother, perhaps, with sainted, tender face, or his wife, with spirit eyes turned eagerly upon him.

What has he done, what has any man done, to deserve this lavishment of love, this wealth of incentive to a manly life? And what can he do, if he is a man, but spurn the baseness that will grieve these presences, and live in some way worthy of their love?

With what endlessness God has endowed our human deeds! It is a divine, an awful attribute. You need be no Demosthenes to speak words that never will die; every man on earth has done that. You need be no Alexander to affix an imperishable stamp upon the universe; every man on earth has done that.

But when God gave wings to our lives, He let them fly down as well as up. Have you not committed some sin, years past, perhaps, that is as terribly on your

Human Dignity

heart as if it were yesterday, that has not left you with its anguish for a single day, that has brought woe to birth upon woe in daily generations of sorrow, and that, unless God hides some Lethe in the after life, will follow you with an eternity of remorse? Praise God, indeed, if you have not many such sins!

For there is not an evil thought, cherished in the blackest of midnight, but may shudder down through all the sorrowing ages. There is not the least temptation, which you embrace however cautiously, but may widen out to the circle of your life and all lives. Bless God, there is no end to goodness. O God, is there no end to sin?

What will you do, then, in the face of this horror? What will you do, then, whose least deed may do so much? What can you do but pray, at all times, and with all your soul:—

O my Creator, I am fearfully and wonderfully made. I stand afraid before myself. I glory in the good Thou hast opened before me, I tremble at my powers of evil. I can go so far at a step, I dare not step without Thee. Since my moments are immortal, I dare not live a moment without Thee. I bring to Thee my wretched past. Thou alone canst overtake the evil word, and silence it. Thou alone canst stay the wave of influence, and level it with the sea. Thou alone canst ransom my soul from the prison of its past. I will walk from my dungeon free, with Thee! I will dare the transformation Thou dost offer, the sceptre, the throne! I will dare the dignity of manhood, I will live as a child of God! And I will do it in humble reliance on Him who was the Son of God and Son of man. Amen.

XII

Help from Vigilance

UST after I have sinned, how easy it is to repent! How decisively I plan never to yield again! How desirable, how attainable, is a life of purity—just after I have sinned!

I find that nothing is easier, or more satisfying, than to devise a way out of temptation; and that nothing is easier, or more humiliating, than to fall in such a way.

I find that the devil's most persuasive sedative is to say, "That is the last time. Henceforth you are God's and not the devil's. Lift up your head and puff out your breast!"

I find that it is the easiest thing in the world to plan how I shall cease sinning. I find that it is the hardest thing in the world—just to stop.

If I could only perpetuate the horror of sin that comes just after I have sinned! If my eyes could always see its real character as I perceive it then! If my heart could always understand its fearful consequences as I comprehend them at that moment! How impossible it seems to sin again—just after I have sinned!

But Satan masks as an angel of light. He is never more at home than in the garb of sham repentance. Little cares he how much straw is thrown away, while the root is in the ground.

Satan undermines like a wave, that retreats after each onset, only to get momentum for a fresh attack.

Satan destroys like an intermittent fever, allowing us, every other day, to renew the confidence of health, that he may seize our powers unaware.

Satan is most to be feared when we fear him not, and most to be avoided when he withdraws from us.

Not once for all did Christ, those forty days in the wilderness, conquer Satan. The adversary left him only "for a season." Many and many a time Christ had to cry, "Get thee behind me, Satan!"

That is why the Master bids us "Watch!" That is why, over and over through the marvelous three years of teaching, He exclaims, "Watch! Ye know not the day nor the hour. He comes like a thief in the night. He sows while ye sleep. Watch, watch, watch!"

Vigilance

As I write, the Government is carrying on its naval manœuvres. Somewhere off the coast of New England is a mimic hostile fleet. The fleet of defense is anxiously anticipating an attack. Its search-lights are ranging the waves for torpedo boats. Its lines of intelligence are flashing up and down the coast. Every harbor is hot with expectation.

For three days the " enemy " have been invisible. The tension is growing desperate. The longer the delay, the more imminent is the assault. But where? The weary hours of watching are beginning to tell. It is a contest of nerves, not of gunpowder. Who will be the first to nod?

Fit symbol, this, of the contest I am waging on the sea of the soul! Only, my ship is but one, and the black fleet of the adversary is multitudinous.

But one? Ah, blind that I am! Open my eyes, Lord, as Thou didst open Elisha's, that I may see the ocean crowded with celestial battleships round about my frail vessel! But one? I am convoyed by all the armament of heaven!

For Thou, O my God, hast an eye that never sleeps. Not from the opening dawn of creation, through all the multitude of midnights since, has Thy vigilance relaxed, Thy soul yielded to slumber.

With what love Thou hast brooded over me! With what passionate care Thou hast sought to warn me of peril! What safeguards hast Thou placed about me! What alarms hast Thou raised! Through what weary, disappointing years has Thy care been unrewarded, Thy watchfulness found me asleep!

Can I not watch with Thee one hour?

It is only an hour, after all. So brief is my life, so short is the vigilance needed.

Only a little time to be a man, and then a glorified spirit forever! Only a little testing, and then eternal assurance! Only a short stress and strain, and then the endless reaches undisturbed!

Can I not watch with Thee one hour?

Can I not, in the first place, get a better memory for my sins? Let me often brood over them, not for discouragement, but for understanding. Let me constantly remind myself how I sinned last time,—how a brief righteousness led to confidence, and confidence to carelessness, and carelessness to a fall. Let me recall the circumstances of the sin, not to gloat over them, but to avoid them. Let me renew from day to day my horror of sin and the ardor of my last repentance.

And, in the second place, can I not build up a barrier against the devil? A barrier of good books, manly exercise, ennobling friendships, purifying prayers. It is not enough for a general to repel attacks. It is possible for him to make a fort so strong that it will not be attacked. It will then stand unworn by conflict and undisturbed by anxiety.

And then, can I not make resistance to evil the rule of my life? Can I not absolutely cease dalliance with it, even in apparent trifles? Can I not engage in some world-wide or nation-wide battle against it, that I may see its hideousness in the large and so come to hate it more heartily in myself? Can I not cease to be a militiaman against the devil, and enlist in the regular army? Can I not abandon amateurdom, and make it a business to abolish sin?

The task requires time. Most men are weak because they will not spend time on their muscles; most men are spiritual weaklings because they will not take time to be holy.

The task requires toil. Vigilance means vigils. A fort is not a hotel. Armies do not carry feather beds. No one can master himself and please himself. Sin is a disease, and there is no room for ease in the conquest of it.

The task requires thought. We are opposed by a master of strategy. No empty brain can beat the devil. There is not an argument, there is not a confirmation of reason, there is not a fortifying of example, there is not a testimony of science, there is not a plea of the sages, there is not a command of Scripture, that will not be needed in the warfare.

I would magnify Satan. For though, matched with our God, he is such a feeble thing, matched with men he is a terrible thing. Sin slumbers not. Sin reaches everywhere. Darkness is light for sin, and the intricacies of the soul are sin's highways. No man is safe against sin, and the omnipresent peril is also infinite and eternal.

How shall I avoid sin unless I fear it? And how shall I fear it unless I hate it? And how shall I hate it unless, with all my horrified being, I know it?

Let me admit no lapse in my hatred, that there may be no flaw in my vigilance. If the devil wears a green

Vigilance

robe, let me even avoid the green trees! If the devil cloaks himself in blue, let me even shun the blue sky!

Let me know that I have fallen when I begin to fall, and not only when I reach the bottom of the pit. Let me know that I am most in danger when I begin to slight the danger. Let me know that silence is all the consent the devil wants, and that drooping eyes are the only opportunity he seeks.

But is the memory of sin to darken all my hours on earth? Better thus, than that the fact of sin should shroud your eternal life.

But is the Christian to know no peace? Yes, peace *in* the conflict; never, on earth, peace *from* the conflict.

What avails the presence of Christ, if Satan also must ever be present to my thought? This, that the devil will be behind you, Christ being ever before you!

How can I pray without ceasing, and watch without intermission, I with my human frailties, I with my fluctuating powers?

You breathe without ceasing: make prayer the breath of your soul! Your heart beats without ceasing: make watchfulness the pulse of your nature!

How can I make prayer my breath and vigilance my heart-beat? for that is a mystical metaphor, and temptations are uncompromising realities.

Ah, then, make prayer a reality, the presence of Christ a reality, the love of purity a reality, the hatred of evil a reality! If sin is more real to you than prayer, it is *to you* it is more real, and not to God's saints. To them, the life of prayer is the only substantial life, and sin has become the half-forgotten horror of a dream.

There is no vigilance against sin until there is sincerity in the Christian life. When we begin—I do not say, to love God with all our heart, but to *try* to love Him with all our heart, then we can begin to fight Satan with all our soul.

And any other antagonism to evil is no antagonism at all. The fort is not guarded, however vigilant the sentries in front, if one sentry at the rear corner falls asleep. Satan prefers the rear and the corners. The soul is not opposing Satan, however brave its show of opposition, while one least desire is in league with him.

Must we then be perfect, in order to become perfect? Aye, as our Father in heaven is perfect! That is the Christian paradox.

Vigilance

It would be a hopeless paradox, were our own perfection the only one attainable. But we may put on Christ. As a seamless robe, His purity. As a flawless armor, His courage. As a garment of light, His vigilance.

Yes, we may put on Christ. In His perfection we may put off the works of darkness and assume the armor of light. Joined with Him, we shall make no more provision for the flesh, to fulfil the lusts thereof.

Come, then, blessed Lord, who art ever watching in Gethsemane! Dwell Thou in us, and we will watch with Thee. Though with agony and bloody sweat, we will watch with Thee. Though in a passion of prayer, we will watch with Thee. Though the darkness deepens and Judas draws near, we will watch with Thee. Though the night is long and cold, though the rocks are hard, though the tempest beats upon us, we will watch with Thee. For the morning will break at last. The sun will rise over Olivet. The birds will sing, and the heavens will shout. For our ascension day will come, and the Father will lift us out of Gethsemane, forever and ever. Amen.

XIII

Help from the Atonement

O one can in his deepest soul believe the atonement unless he has set himself to the desperate struggle with sin, has fallen and risen again, once more fallen again to rise, and so lived in alternate courage and despair. The atonement is not a truth that angels can comprehend; only sad, discouraged, shamefaced man.

For no one can fight long against his sin without discovering that it is not to-day's sin alone that he is combating, but yesterday's sin also, and last year's. If it were only to-day's sin, the contest would be hard enough; but when it has back of it the downward momentum of all past sins, the battle is indeed a terrible one.

For there never was a sin that did not make the next sin easier to commit, just as flames grow upon flames, or mildew upon mildew.

I am master of to-day, but yesterday is master of me. I have strength enough to meet to-day's temptations—perhaps; at least, no one has more than enough strength for that. Certainly I have not strength enough to fight, in addition to to-day's temptations, the temptations of last month, of the last decade.

Yet how they swarm upon me! The poison my soul imbibed, from book or picture or spoken word, a dozen years ago. The evil habit I formed, perhaps, in my childhood. The brandied air that burst out upon me yesterday as I passed a certain door. The memory of a wrong, forgotten by every one else, that has rankled in my heart for twenty years, embittered my life and bent it toward unkindness. I can forget the good; why is it so hard to forget the evil?

Temptations are derelicts; they are dismantled wrecks of pirate ships, floating on the ocean of life. They have been met and fought and overcome, but they are as dangerous thus adrift as they ever were when the crew was aboard and all sails were set. I am likely to run into them at any time.

Oh, the awful power of an evil past! Oh, the horror of any evil in a past however good! Memory has wings for any height. Memory can see in any darkness. Memory can follow any course of fortune. And suggestions of wickedness often grow more fascinating with time, like the ripening apples in the Garden of Eden.

Oh, the awful power of an evil past! Oh, the horror of any evil in a past however good! It is always lurking around the corner. It may leap out of any shadow. As infection may lie in the dust along a rafter, to repeat and multiply the disease after the physicians are forgotten, so sin lies in poisonous ambush.

Oh, the awful power of an evil past! Oh, the horror of any evil in a past however good! Men may raise a dyke against the ocean, but not against the tide of memory. Men may erect a barrier against the wind, but not against the miasma of a remembered passion. Men may drain a swamp, but no tiles can be laid along the corrugations of the brain.

"I live," the sinner must say, in horrible echo of Paul's words, " I live, yet not I, but sin living in me. The poisonous vapor I once drew in is still the breath of my life. The devil's tool I once used is still the habit of my hand. I am, sadly and fearfully, all that I have been."

But the evil past is more than a living memory, a perpetuated temptation; it is an accumulating penalty.

Those that are fighting sin—I say not, those that sin, but those that are fighting sin—need no proof that sin is punished. No surer the char after the

the Atonement

fire, no surer the rot after the mildew, no surer the dissolution after the consumption, than penalty after sin.

No need to say, " Eternity will prove it," for time proves it, the next instant exemplifies it.

No need to say, " Eternity will continue it," for every year adds to its power, the swiftness and black depth of its current.

No need to say, " It is inevitable," for they have been using all arts to shun it, and they see the world of sinners with every sin using all arts to shun it, yet it comes, and comes instantly, and comes increasingly.

What life is there, however fair to the eye, over which is not stamped the black doom, " Forfeit!" " Forfeit " because of a myriad misdeeds. " Forfeit" to eternal death.

I do not say that all sinners feel this; far from that. Millions revolt against the justice of God's decrees. Millions assert that they are not so much to blame, that they are the sport of fate, the creatures of circumstance, the victims of their irresponsible nature. Millions deny that any penalty is their desert, save perhaps the transient punishment of weakness, loss, disease, or discomfort here in the body.

But I do say that all sinners that have earnestly struggled against their sin feel this. They comprehend their iniquity. They realize how deeply it is seated, how persistently ingrained. They loathe themselves. They themselves have long ago written " Forfeit " upon their souls. They know that they are lost.

Looking backward, they see the on-rolling wave of transgressions, rushing with cumulative velocity down the slopes of time. Looking around, they see the present duty, and themselves barely able to do it, daily weaker against the crescent might of temptation and growing dread of doom. Looking ahead into the lowering future they see no light, for the sun is buried behind them.

These are only words to the careless, only fancies to the scoffer, only hypocrisies to the hardened; but to the awakened sinner, who is yet bound to the body of his death, I have painted the picture true.

And so I cannot paint—no words can describe—the joy the atonement brings to such a soul. He alone, as I say, can believe it. It soon becomes the one Belief to him.

That the past can be rolled up, sealed, and sunk in the bottomless pit!

the Atonement

That the past can be washed out, its stains removed, its foulnesses made white as snow!

That the past can be transformed, taken up into the illimitable Divine, its very atoms disassociated and recombined, till the long, wrong years have become a new creation, fit for a new creature!

That the flood of iniquitous memories can be barred. That the derelicts can be sunk. That the floating germs can be captured and destroyed. That man cannot do it, but that it can be done.

That God will remember our sins no more. And if they no longer exist in God's memory, they cannot exist in any memory.

This is the atonement. This is the Gospel, the Good News.

It is news indeed. We could never have guessed it. Without the Life, we could never have believed it.

For we cannot understand it. There is but one atonement, but there are scores of theories of it. And those comprehend it best who do not try to understand it, only accept it.

It is to be accepted without understanding because it comes from Him whom we must accept, yet cannot understand.

From Him who surely lived and died and rose again; from Him who ruled waves and wind, trees, animals, diseases, death; from Him who spake as never man spake; from Him whom the ages had foretold, to whom the opening heavens testified; from Him who was tempted in all points as we are, yet without sin.

It was He who promised eternal life to all that should believe Him. It was He whose very name means Saviour. It was He whose blood was shed for the sending away of sins. It was He, the living Bread, of whom if one eat he will live forever. It was He through whose sacrifice our sins, though scarlet, shall be as white as snow; and though red like crimson, they shall be as wool. Praise to His blessed name forever!

There is truth in all theories of the atonement. It is too vast a truth to be comprehended by all theories; its margins reach far beyond them. Live in the atonement, if you want to see how much more we know than we understand.

And you will live in the atonement if you simply accept it, and place it among the undoubted facts of your life. If you simply say, " Here is Christ, very man, very God. I believe Him. I love Him. I adore Him. Here are His

the Atonement

words, that from all that believe Him He will remove their iniquity, and remember it no more forever. I believe Him. Those words are true of me."

Then, if you really believe this, you will live in that belief; your life will be that belief.

Do I mean that your old evil life will no longer steal through the doors of memory and the gates of habit, that the temptations of the past will be temptations no longer?

Perhaps. Many a drunkard, whom gold cures and all other cures had dismally failed to cure, has lost on conversion his appetite for alcohol; many a licentious man has forgotten his lusts, many a covetous man has got rid of his greed.

But also, perhaps not. There are converted drunkards to whom the odor of a bar is still a maddening allurement. There are converted debauchees and misers who must always, in this life, fight their lusts.

And do I mean that the penalty of sin is altogether removed? No, not that, either. If the drunkard has ruined his digestion, conversion will not restore his health. If the miser has driven a debtor to a wretched grave, conversion will not restore the debtor to life.

What, then, is the atonement good for?

This: greatly, this: it puts us at one with God. So that we count it all joy when we fall into manifold temptations, gladly acquiescing in God's plans for our discipline and testing. So that we become a part of God's justice, and exult in the reign of His righteousness, and would not have rebellion against Him less severely punished, though it were to remove heavy sorrow from ourselves.

At one with God! He dwelling in us and we in Him. His future our future. His safety our safety. His purity our purity. His peace our peace. If I have this, what can I wish besides? What, indeed, is there besides to wish?

I do not ask it, my Saviour. I receive it. I will not study it. I will use it. I am done with the past, now Thou hast begun with it. I will forget my sins, remembering Thee. I welcome the life Thou dost send me. It is Thy life now, and to be welcomed with exultation. Press the temptations in at every point. It is Thy life. So did Satan assail Thee. So did the thorns pierce Thy flesh. Weigh me down with the merited penalties of my transgressions. It is Thy life. So, all undeserving, wert Thou weighed down in Gethsemane, on Calvary. Shall the disciple be more blest than his Lord, the redeemed than the Redeemer? So shall I walk with Thee on the earth. So shall I reign with Thee in glory. And walking or reigning my joy shall be in Thee, Lord Jesus. Amen.

XIV

Help from the Bible

OU have a Bible; but do you own it? You hold it in your hands; do you hold it in your heart? You read in it; do you feed on it?

The Bible is the medicine-chest given us by the Great Physician. Are the labels on the sixty-six vials eloquent to you? Do you know for what each is a remedy, or do you take them at haphazard and in the dark?

There are two primary mistakes with regard to the Bible. One is not to read it at all; the other is not to read it with a purpose.

And so there are two primary directions for the use of the Bible. One is, Read it. Read it regularly, read it perseveringly, read it in large measure, perhaps a book at a time. The other is, Always read it for power. Power over doubt, power over grief, power over temptation.

Tempted souls have gone to the Bible, opened it at ignorant random, and hit upon a vein of the gold they sought.

The Bible

For the Bible is rich in precious ore. But others have blundered upon no discovery, and have scouted the Bible as a useless book.

Not thus does the wise gold-seeker go to work. He prospects the mountains, valley after valley, spur after spur, peak after peak. He learns the strata, what they are, how they lie, what each contains. To this he goes for lead, to that for zinc, to another for silver. He could guide you along any path in the dark, and when he strikes pick, it is not in vain.

So it is with this mountain range of the Bible. A friend may point out one rich outcropping or two, but it is only a shift for the time. You must know the Bible through and through, for yourself.

No one knows whether the Bible can help him or not until he has read it from cover to cover, in sections large enough to give comprehensive views, with aids sufficient to insure understanding, and with a definite purpose systematically pursued. In no inferior fashion would you survey a farm offered for sale; and surely the Bible has as much promise for you as a farm.

Therefore, O tempted soul, book after book, from Genesis to Revelation, pursue the sacred journey! Tarry not with the beauties and delights that crowd upon you. Keep an eye single for one discovery,—help against temptation.

And wherever you find this help, plainly mark it in the margin, returning to the spot over and over, and reviewing its wisdom till it has joined itself to your soul.

If you read the Bible with this one aim, there are few pages you will not mark; just as there are few pages you will not mark if you read the Bible with any other aim.

From the fall of man in the opening chapters to the doom of the wicked and reward of the righteous in the closing chapter, the entire Bible is a treatise on temptation and its conquest. The stories of Adam, Eve, Cain, and Noah; of Abraham, Lot, Esau, and Jacob; of Joseph, Moses, Miriam, and Aaron; of Balaam, Joshua, Samson, and Gideon; of Eli, Samuel, Saul, David, Absalom, and Solomon; of Rehoboam, Jeroboam, Ahab, and Elijah; of Esther, Ezra, Nehemiah, Jeremiah, and Daniel; of Amos and Micah; of John the Baptist and Jesus our Lord; of Mary, of Magdalene, of Judas, Peter, and Paul—all the names I have named, and scores of names I might add, are pictured in the Bible as conquerors or victims of temptation.

It was prophesied of John the Baptist that he should live in the spirit and power of Elijah; and he did. So may all who will read the Bible live in the spirit and power of John and Elijah both, and of all the other men and women of God, who have overcome themselves and the world.

It is possible, reading and thinking long of a noble character, to incorporate his personality in our lives; it is not only possible, it is inevitable. You have read your Bible to little purpose unless you, too, become an Elijah, a John the Baptist.

You will never know what portion of the wonderful book will aid you most, or next. I remember that once I was greatly helped in temptation by reading the story of the woman who touched Christ's robe in the crowd. To this day, though it was years ago, I can feel the thrill with which I realized that the slightest contact of faith with Christ would heal me of my sin.

Many another passage has come to me, at the time of need, with a message as fresh and startling as if God had spoken from the air above my head. Yet they might all be ineffective in your temptations, while your discoveries might be meaningless to me.

For no man owns the whole Bible. It is too large for that, and our experience is too small. Every man makes his own Bible—a Bible constantly growing, if he grows, but always a smaller Bible than the Scriptures.

It is a great thing to make a Bible—one of the greatest things any man ever does. For no one can make a Bible except through making his own, one by one, the experiences of the Bible heroes and saints. Did any one ever add all the Psalms to his Bible? or all of the letter to the Romans?

The Bible you make is the only one you can really use. It is not using a passage to hunt it up with a concordance and dig out its meaning with a commentary, any more than it is using your house to prove title in a court of law. You use your house when you live in it, and so with a Bible passage.

And what a lordly palace the Bible is! There are rooms we never enter. There are ranges of rooms that are as unfamiliar as a stranger's house. How little of our Bibles we have really moved into!

It was only the other day that I moved into First and Second Corinthians. Just now they are my favorite rooms. I am still in the new delight of discovery of those twelve connected galleries, the

Minor Prophecies. And in every room I find surprises of usefulness and beauty all the time.

It is easy to think that you are making a Bible when you are not. No Bible is yours till you use it. You do not use it until it has become an instinct.

You do not use your Bible if, when you are tempted, you must say to yourself, " Now is there anything in Paul's writings that fits this temptation? Let me see—Romans, Corinthians First, Second, a, e, i, o, Galatians, Ephesians, Philippians, Colossians; perhaps the armor chapter would fit; I will look it up." Satan would deal his decisive stroke long before that.

No; you are using Paul's writings if, as soon as the temptation assails you, your thought leaps to its weapons: " Keep the body under! Mortify the flesh! Crucified with Christ! With the temptation the way of escape! In all points tempted like as we are! Stand, therefore! Resist unto blood, striving against sin!" This is to be a Paul and to own his writings, that is to say, his spirit and power.

A paper Bible will not answer; only a memory Bible will avail in the combat with the devil. He likes best to fight in the darkness, when you cannot see to read; in your feebleness, when you are too weary to hunt up a book; in your despondency, when heart and will are broken.

Sin flashes upon you through your instincts, the baser ones; therefore I say the Bible cannot help you till it also has become an instinct, a holy one.

How shall we exalt the Bible into an instinct? Only by meditation and obedience.

By meditation. No hasty wooing wins a great truth. If you want the Bible you must pay the price, and part of the price is time and patience. A lifetime of courageous living is in the six pages of Amos, and will you make them your own in half an hour?

And by obedience. No one has a larger Bible than he obeys. No one can enlarge his Bible except by obeying more. That story of the woman who touched Christ's garment is yours only as you also reach out the finger of faith. Paul's armor is yours only as you engage in Paul's battles.

To think about the Bible so much that we cannot help thinking about it, and obey it so heartily that obedience becomes a habit,—this is the way to make the Bible a help in temptation.

It is a noble art—that of meditation. To start out in the day with some magnificent thought, like Paul's "I buffet my body." To recur to it, in the interstices of work and play. To reason with ourselves, "Now, what did Paul mean by that? What experiences led him to it? How did he illustrate it? What literal meaning has it for me? What spiritual significance? Have I done it? Am I doing it? If not, why not, and how can I do it?" To talk about it with one's friends. To look for accidental sidelights upon it, such as are sure to come. To review it all at night, and ask God's blessing upon it, and His Spirit to lead you still further into its truth,—all this is only a hint of the business of meditation.

And it is a still more noble art,—that of obedience. The obedience that does not bandy arguments, or palter, or postpone. The obedience that listens eagerly and with poised powers. The obedience that exults in the authority back of the command and is proud of a post under it. The obedience that leaps and laughs. Our age of silly independence knows little of this, as, in its silly bustle, it knows little of meditation.

The more one meditates, the better he meditates and the more rejoicingly. The more one obeys, the better he obeys and the more happily. Make but a purposeful beginning, and you will soon make your Bible and your life.

And yet is meditation all? Are meditation and obedience all? Lacking one thing, meditation thinks a man into no truth, but into the bog. Lacking one thing, obedience falls into the first pit of despondency. That one thing is the presence of the Holy Spirit of God.

Ever, therefore, as you open the lids of your Bible, pray in your deepest heart this prayer:—

Revealer! Guide! Encourager! Confirmer of purpose and of power! The truth is Thine and of Thee, and Thou alone canst lead me into it. The way is Thine and to Thee, and Thou alone canst direct me in it. The hope is Thine and for Thee, and Thou alone canst assure me of it. Will and strength are of Thy creation, formed to bend toward Thee, and Thou alone knowest how to uphold them. Speak to me, Infinite Friend, out of these leaves of the past. Make each one of them vital with Thy voice. Make each one of them personal to my need. Take of the things of Christ and show them to me. Be my memory, Thou mindful Spirit! Be my readiness, Thou that never failest! Be my confidence, Thou that seest the end from the beginning, and beyond these tempests of temptation the meadows of heaven. In Thy name of majesty and love. Amen.

XV

Help from Prayer

CAN you be on the water and the land at the same time? Can you at the same time rise into the ether and fall into the pit? No more can you truly pray, and, while praying, yield to temptation.

The physician, as he enters the smallpox ward, surrounds himself with an atmosphere that is proof against the dread disease. Such an atmosphere, proof against the hideous peril of sin, is prayer.

You may think that your experience disproves this. You may remember the many, many times when, with the foul breath of sin in your face and its polluting fascination luring you on, you have panted out, "O God! Save me, O God!" and yet have gone on sinning.

But the fact that you have gone on sinning proves that you were not praying. For no one sins unless he wishes to sin; it is the wish that is the sin. And no one prays unless he yearns toward God; that yearning is the prayer. And not until light and darkness fill the same space at the same time can the human heart seek God and Satan simultaneously.

It is easy to pretend to pray. It is so easy to fool ourselves with our prayers! It is so impossible to deceive God!

Words are not prayer, though from night till morning you groan, "Deliver me from temptation." Desires toward God may not be prayer; it depends upon the kind of desires they are.

It is not prayer to feel ashamed, before God and men. It is not prayer to be sorry for the consequences of sin. It is not prayer to wish release from the consequences of sin. All three of these moods may be upon us even while we are sinning, but the praying mood may never be upon us while we are sinning.

For prayer is a reaching out toward God; and toward God is always away from sin.

Do I then make prayer impossible for you while you remain a lover of sin? Yes, I do.

But do you not need prayer to redeem you from the love of sin and bring you into the love of God? Yes, you do. The natural heart is enmity against God, and only supernatural means, only prayer, can transform it into love of God, which is prayer.

Then do I not make it impossible for you to redeem yourself from temptation and sin through prayer? Precisely; it is impossible.

Else why the Redeemer? Else why the Cross? Else why the Intercession of the Son with the Father? Else why the Groanings of the Holy Spirit, pleading for us with unutterable desire? Why? Because we could not, cannot, do these things for ourselves.

Because the drowned man cannot lift himself from the bottom of the sea. Because the dead soul cannot bring itself to life. Prayer is life, and we are dead—dead in trespasses and sins.

You will not appreciate prayer—its majesty, its power, its loveliness—until you understand the divine origin of it. There never was a human prayer, however faltering and feeble and brief, but was prompted and made possible by God. Even the prayer, " Lord, teach us to pray!" is Christ-inspired.

Is there, then, no merit in our prayers? None whatever. The very breath of pride, of spiritual complacency, is fatal to a prayer.

And are prayers, then, accidental? Must we wait for God to impel us? Are we prayer automata, mere puppets of a worship-seeking Jehovah? And how can a prayer make us better if it is not spontaneous?

Brother, it is! Nothing in all the world is so spontaneous, voluntary, independent, as a prayer. It is the conditions only that God provides, and He provides them constantly. Prayer possibilities, unceasing and numberless as the waves of sunlight, He wraps around us. We live—even the worst of us lives—in an atmosphere of invitations to prayer.

But we may shut out the sunshine, and we may repel these invitations. Prayer is communion with God. We cannot go to God. God comes hourly to us. But we may close our eyes and our ears and our lips.

"Behold, I stand at the door and knock." That is the Christian's call to prayer! That is the pathos of prayer—God's yearning, so often repulsed. That is the power of prayer,—it is based, not on our weak human desires, but on the desires of an infinite God.

Ship-wrecked soul, storm-beaten and despairing! Arms are around you as you sink—arms of the Lord of the

Isles. His harbor is at hand. His palace is warm. His feast is bright. Yes, His arms are around you as you sink; why do you beat them back? Lean upon them, just lean upon them, and that will be prayer.

The very temptation, the very storm and peril of your soul, is an invitation to prayer. Your very helplessness, your hopelessness, is an invitation to prayer. The mute terror with which you sink among the waves is an invitation to prayer. For underneath are the everlasting arms.

Prayer is not a wrestling with God, as Jacob wrestled with the angel of the covenant. Jacob did not so wrestle; the angel wrestled with him. The tempted soul, enervated by sin, is too weak to wrestle; but it is not too weak to cling.

Learn, then, to trust God for prayer, as you trust Him for everything else. It would be strange indeed if you could not without His help bring a single seed to life, while this greatest of all events, life-bestowing communion with the Most High, you could avail to bring about!

And trust God in prayer. That rapt devotion, that ecstasy of bliss, that assurance of faith, that celestial sweep of spirit, which you have read about and heard about from God's saints, are gifts from God. They may not be for you.

God fulfils Himself in many ways. He comes to John in clouds of glory. He comes to Peter in a cloth full of common food.

In prayer never consider your feelings; prayer is far more real and important than your feelings, because prayer is the feeling of God.

You have only two things to know, if you would be rescued by prayer from your temptations. Your soul must be persuaded of the hatefulness of sin and of the loveliness of God. And the two knowledges are one.

There are only two motions in the sinner's prayer,—away from sin, and toward God. And the two motions are one.

The problem of prayer, then, is twofold—to learn to hate sin, to learn to love God. You may begin at either end, or at both ends.

Only, know this, that if you love sin you cannot pray, and if you do not love God you cannot pray, and you do not love God unless you hate sin.

I have defined prayer as the love of God. Do not let men confuse you with non-essentials and impertinences,— the words of prayer, whether many or few, vocal or inaudible; the time of prayer, the length of prayer, the frequency of prayer. Love God with all your heart, and you will pray perfect prayers. You cannot help it.

I have exalted prayer as the specific against sin. I have shown its dependence upon the atonement, how it is the atonement, in present, personal operation. I have shown how simple it is, and how sure. But all this is less than the wind among the dry leaves—unless we pray.

Unless we resolve to know God, and to know sin no more. Unless, though we have only a fibre of strength, we use it to turn us away from sin. Unless, though we have only the fragment of a desire for purity, we nourish that fragment. Unless, though we can see but the dim outline of God, we press toward that imperfect vision, and, though we can hear only a few words of His great voice, we answer what we hear.

Begin to pray. Begin now to pray. Rather, accept the beginning of prayer that has always existed from God toward you.

Nothing else so large as prayer grows from so small a seed. Prayer is a bit of worthless paper presented at a great bank by a pauper—presented, and honored for a princely fortune!

Have no thought of your worth or your worthlessness. Forget your sins, as you forget your virtues. Forget even, if it is possible, the temptations against which you pray. Forget everything, but God.

As a preparation for prayer, crowd your life with thoughts of God. Yonder cloud—God impels it. This tree—God built it. My hand—God fashioned it, in likeness to His hand. A slice of bread—thank Thee, Father! Some one's merry smile—that was a reflection from God's face.

Read about God, study about God, talk about God, hear about God, meditate on God, persistently, systematically, and lavishly, as a preparation for prayer.

Yet do not wait for any preparation. Begin to pray. Begin now to pray. Think of God, waiting to talk with you. Remember who He is—the invisible Creator of all seen things, the unfailing Upholder of all trustful things, Supreme of supremacies, Origin of wisdom, Lover of lovers. And remember that, whether your heart turns toward Him or not, His is always eagerly pulsing for you.

Oh, with your contrition, with your despair of yourself, with your dread of the future, chained to sin as you are

Prayer

and kissing your chains, and loathing yourself as you kiss, ought it to be hard to pray, you as you are, and God as He is?

It need not be a grand prayer, but only a simple one and short:—

Dear Father, what am I, that Thou shouldst let me talk with Thee! It is for Thee to say how long I shall bear Thee, and how close I shall come to Thee. How weak I am Thou knowest, how depraved. I will not tell Thee, for Thou knowest. Tell me how strong Thou art, how pure. Sing to my soul the triumph of the Cross. If Thou wouldst abide with Zacchæus, so with me. If Thou wouldst receive a sinner's ointment, receive mine. If Thou wouldst tarry with the Samaritan, sit by me at the well. If Thou didst come to seek and to save the lost, come now to me. Even so come, Lord Jesus. Amen.

XVI

Help from Out-of-Doors

I AM writing this upon a hilltop. There is spread before me a sunny expanse, stretching for many miles, and crowded with the beauties of God. There is the near slope of grass, gay with aster and goldenrod. Below, there are trees and bushes, tangles of green hung with scarlet berries and purple beach-plums. Beyond, there is the sparkling blue of the ocean, broken up by the daintiest of islands. Above, a flawless heaven.

Motion is here, the swaying branches, the bending grassblades, the long marching of the waves, their bayonets glittering in the sun. Fragrance is here, of the pines and of the salt sea. Color is here, all the kaleidoscopic hues of autumn. Sound is here, the shrill monotone of crickets, the varied greetings of the wind, the dropping notes of a song sparrow. Form is here, no two alike of leaf or flower or bird or wave. And all —motion, fragrance, color, sound, and form—all are subdued to a single harmony, pervasive and persuasive; which must be the thought of God.

While I am here upon this hill of splendor, how far from my mind is the thought of sin! The ocean has washed it all away, the sunlight has laughed it away, the birds have sung it away, the breezes have borne it off on viewless pinions, and if a hint of it were left, the pure loveliness that surges around me would overwhelm it, forty fathoms deep.

I am not tempted to sin while I am in the woods, or under the solemn stars. By a long walk or a long row I can distance any temptation. A day with God among the mountains energizes me for many a day with Satan in the city.

But may not God be found in the city and under roofs? Assuredly, yes. And is God always found among the hills? Assuredly, no. The heart is God's home, and not the ocean or the forest. Sin, and not a brick wall, separates us from God.

And is not the church God's house, where He loves best to be found? Though "the woods were God's first temples," are they His latest and best? Assuredly, though God dwells not in temples made with hands, and the meeting-house stones are no more sacred than hearthstones, yet where two or three are gathered in His name, Christ is in the midst.

It is those that find God most in the church that most find Him out of the church. Jehovah has no quarrel with Himself, Mount Zion with Olivet. The wise man will seek God everywhere, and the tempted man must.

Examining my own life and the lives of others, I find that the devil is sedentary. He hates the open. He loves darkness rather than light, and rooms rather than sky. He closes the windows. He clogs the feet with leather and binds the lungs with steel and silk. He invents gluttony and sofas. Out-of-doors is too wide and sweet for him.

Review your temptations and your sins of the past. Have you yielded and fallen when penetrated with the cheery sunshine, or was it under the shallow rays of gas and electricity? Has the sin mastered you when your lungs were crammed with the ozone of the shore, or when they were smothered in the heavy air of a ballroom? Have evil fancies made nests in your brain after an hour of woodland rambles among the birds, or after an hour's reading of some incestuous tale?

Out-of-doors is energetic. God's world is at work. From ant to oak, from rivulet to cloud, from violet to mountain, all is activity. Those that live much in the open catch the mighty pulse-beat of God.

What an ally is physical ardor in the contest with sin! Pure blood is not unrelated to a pure heart. A strong circulation has to do with a sturdy consecration. Stout muscles help lift the soul over spiritual bogs, and a good constitution has some connection with a good conscience.

Out-of-doors is pure. Human picture galleries reek with poisonous suggestions, but you might tread forever the majestic corridors of the woods, and find no curve, no color, no glimpse, that ministers to passion. Human music is often sensuous, but the music of the forest, the sea, and the sky is an echo of the music in heaven. Human libraries have preserved the baseness as well as the nobility of men, but every page of the book of nature is white and sweet.

Why pray, " Lead me not into temptation," while you turn your feet where temptation has many times assailed you? The woods are safe, the crowds are unsafe. You know how slight a spark will kindle the red fire within you. Why live among blazing torches?

Out-of-doors is peaceful. Even the raging of a tempest is a calm beside a frenzied soul. As I write, the sun is sinking across the bay. The ocean receives in motionless reverence his final benediction. The birds are hushed and the breezes are still. This hilltop must be a terraced altar, and spirits innumerable are kneeling around me. Now it is over. The processional of the day has passed, and night has entered upon her tender ritual.

It is over, yet it is not over. The majestic ceremonial has entered my heart. It has filled it, and will abide. While it remains, there will be no room for devils.

And the world has so many hilltops! Room upon them for all earth's tempted millions! For the sun can be seen from any street, and the stars from any window, and there is no level of earth but is a promontory into the universe.

Christ was preaching to an out-of-door people. Most of His disciples were fishermen. Most of His discourses were spoken on hilltops, in meadows, on the streets, or by the sea. Most of them were applications and interpretations of nature. His miracles were not parlor miracles or sickroom miracles. He did not bid His followers live much in the open air, because He did not need to. Most men so lived in that day and country.

What is true of Christ's teachings is true of the entire Bible. It is a book of the fields, the mountains, river, lake, and sky. It does not preach outdoor life, because, in almost every page, it presupposes it.

And I am sure that Christ, if He were to return in the flesh to our modern world, would urge upon men, as one of the needful steps away from temptation and sin, a simpler life. " Ye turn night into day," He would exclaim, " and day into night. Your bodies, temples of the Holy Spirit, ye have imprisoned in effeminacy, luxury, and indolence. Ye barter the sky for a ceiling, sunshine for a lamp, the league-long sweep of the wind for a ventilator. The earth was given you to possess. Ye mortgage it, and bury yourselves in your counting-rooms. Ye have built up an artificial life, and loaded yourselves with artificial needs. Ye have set up in every city a thousand shrines for Satan. Ye have invented temptations that not even he has discovered. And your lives have grown so complex, so hurried, so selfish, and so anxious, that they have no time to fight the devil or worship God."

Somewhat thus, I think, our Lord would speak His rebuke. And I think He would add a command like this: " O ye weary and heavy-laden, raise no heavier burdens than nature binds upon you! O ye tempted ones, ye spirits softened with insidious wiles, ye men that are slaves to a fraction of your being or a fragment of the world, break your bonds, and live out in the largeness of God! Learn anew the elemental pleasures. Breathe in the calmness of the seasons. Subdue your ambitions to the day, and test your passions by the stars. Spread out your thoughts along the meadows, that air and sun may whiten them. Join the anthem of praise that rises from the whole creation. Be a man, as simply, truly, and cheerily as a sparrow is a sparrow or a rose a rose. See God without you as well as within you, and without you that you may see Him within you. For the world is not God, but it is God's, and formed to show you the Father."

And this command, my brother in temptation, which is Christ's, I am sure, as sure as if it were written in the Bible itself,—how shall we go about to obey it? How shall we gain, for our struggle with temptation, the aid of God in nature?

Not without time. We must be content with shorter money-getting, briefer book-revels, fewer indoor delights. We must measure our beds by our needs, and not by our desires. We must plan for out-of-doors, reserve time for it, introduce method and system, and count it a first claim upon our twenty-four hours.

Not without pains. Out-of-doors is not to be wooed from a rocking chair or a landau. Out-of doors is often cold and dark and wet. Before the mountain-top is the toilsome ascent, before the sunrise the leap from a warm bed, before the inner mysteries of the forest are swamps and thickets.

Not without patience. Nature does not blab her secrets to every comer. She demands long waitings at her shrine. Especially, if one comes late to her, with his senses worn by the grinding of worldliness, is she loth to reveal her deeper charms.

But whoever, with simple confidence in God and the desire to know Him better, with absolute horror of sin and the desire to escape from temptation into purity, will live much out-of-doors, into his life will come, soon or late, a sturdy peace and a vital purity that will renovate it wholly, and present it clean and strong for the indwelling of God.

But I have said that one must go to nature in the love of God. One must see in nature more than the natural, or no help will come for the supernatural conflict with evil. A tree is a dead thing; a tree with the thought of Christ is a life-giving thing.

So that here, too, in the beautiful, brave out-of-doors, we set up our oratory and pray our prayer :—

God of nature! Christ, the revealer of God in nature! Holy Spirit, who art daily taking of the things of Christ, in sea, and air, and forest as well as in the Book, and showing them to trusting hearts,—I worship Thee, one God, in all Thy forms and persons! The lovely earth is so full of Thee! And everywhere Thy fulness is grace, and purity, and strength. These presences destroy my evil passions and cleanse my life from its impurity. I would know Thee more, and more perfectly. I would live with Thee more, and more heartily. Not to shun my duty among men, but that I may do it better, I would sometimes go away from men. And when I see a charm in cloud or brook or copse, I shall remember that the Creator is fairer still. And when from ocean or mead or mountain crest the peace of nature steals into my troubled soul, I shall remember that it is only the outer fringe of Christ's garment of peace, which the world cannot give or take away. To that peace, through all Thy blessed agencies, conduct me, O my Saviour, and all Thy tempted children. Amen.

XVII

Help from Recreation

"RECREATION" means "*re-creation*," and surely that is what the tempted soul needs. "Create in me a clean heart, O God, and renew a right spirit within me."

To be renewed in mind, the old desires taken away and new desires substituted, holy, strong, and happy,—for this every tempted man longs, though often unconsciously.

But not every recreation re-creates. Some are named in folly. Call not that a recreation from which you come with aching eyes, burning head, frantic pulse, languid muscles, seared soul. Call not that a re-creation which discreates.

Indeed, it seems like mockery to point a tempted man to recreation as a medicine, while within so many sports lurks the very poison of temptation from which he flees.

Nevertheless it is true that thousands of men go the devil's way for lack of innocent amusements. "All work and no play makes Jack a dull boy," and often a sinful one.

When a spring is wound up all the time it soon loses its tension, and the machine it controls works poorly. That masterful machine, the body, has one mastering need, relaxation. So is it with the supreme machine, the soul.

Satan exults in tension,—the fierce stress of passion, pride, lust, greed, ambition, hatred, fear, worry. Satan never unbends. He does not know how to play. The lord of " gaming," a true game is a mystery to him. As soon as the devil gets into an amusement—for proof look where you will—it becomes hard work, and dis-creating.

This, then, is the decisive test of a recreation: does it re-create? Does one come from it with rested nerves, fresh enthusiasm for work, new joy in life, restored fellowship with men, and a spirit washed clean for converse with God? All this—in differing measure—true recreation will effect. The precise opposite of all this a false recreation will certainly bring about.

Oh, the blessedness of games! Happy is the man who has his quiver full of them! Each is a very pointed arrow, aimed sure at the breast of moroseness, gloom, and laxity, and driving them headlong to their holes!

Recreation

Some men who are called very good cannot play games. Inveigled into an hour with dominoes, draughts, or chess, with tiddledywinks, crokinole, halma, or ping-pong, while others roar with laughter, their stiff lips unbend only in a sarcastic sneer. Such ado over bits of wood or empty rubber balls!

Do you know, I question the goodness of such men. I wonder if, back of their austere uprightness, there does not lurk some eating sin. And anyway, if this uncharitable suspicion is altogether false, I am sure that their attitude toward recreation gives Satan a ready opening for his shafts of temptation.

Why is it that a man is more easily tempted if he does not play? Because his mind, never healthfully unbending, lacks the force needed to ward off temptation. Because his mind, untrained in the bright fencing of games, lacks the alertness needed for the combat with temptation. Because his spirit, unsmoothed with the peace that is born of relaxation, is seized upon more readily by the devil's hooks.

"But," say some objectors, "are not these qualities—force, alertness, peace—the product of religion? And do you not discredit religion when you send us to recreation for them? If a man has the companionship of God, does he need any other recreation?"

Ah, my brothers, how you narrow religion to a pew-width! Why, if you follow Christ, you must go to Cana festivities, to feasts with publicans and sinners! The writings of Paul himself—think of it!—are not devoid of the pun. For example, on that most serious subject, "*so* to think as to think *so*-berly!" Through all centuries the great preachers have left behind them as many exhilarating anecdotes as uplifting sermons.

Recreation is a part of my religion. The two words are alike. Re-ligion is a re-ligature, a binding of the soul back to God, just as re-creation is a re-fashioning of the soul in the image of God wherein it was created. "Recreation" is a better name for the fact than "religion" itself. The church is missing a prime duty as well as a choice opportunity, when it takes toward recreation a position merely negative and prohibitory, and not positive and constructive.

Amusement serves many religious purposes, and none more important than this defeat of temptation. An evening of innocent fun is valid insurance against an impure night. A burst of merry laughter is deadly artillery against the hosts of hell.

Happy the man who is catholic in amusements. Learn to like all innocent games. Play "feathers" with the

Recreation

little children, and croquet with the maidens and young men, and chess with Granther Brown. One needs to play so much and the chances to play are so few, that the wise man will accept any happy invitation.

But though you play many games, select a few for mastery. "No profit goes where there's no pleasure ta'en," and no pleasure is taken in uniform defeat, any more than in uniform and too easy victory. Become a proud expert in golf or tennis, in cycling or canoeing, in photography or microscopy, in chess or checkers.

And you must be an expert in more than one game; select two, the first for daylight and outdoors and the body, the second for indoors and evening and the mind. Tennis and chess make a good combination, according to my thinking; or cycling and—crokinole.

Yes, and the outdoor recreation must be more than one, unless the one can be played in all weathers and at all times of the year,—like that noble recreation, walking.

What I want to insist upon is a plan, method, system. Haphazard recreation is as witless as haphazard creation. You have two razors, and rest one for half the time. Can you not be as prudent with those keenest of all edged tools, your body and your mind?

Play must be planned for as well as work. It is not obtained, in this workaday world, unless it is planned for. And to little purpose, in the end, is your planning for work unless you also plan for play.

It will need patience and perseverance. I have named no amusement—I could not name a healthful amusement—that would not seem tame and stale to a soul that is fevered with sin. How flat is milk to the drunkard!

But let reason reign. Believe others when they tell you of the delights of this sport and that. Perceive the purity and buoyancy it gives them. Take your play as medicine till you can take it with an appetite. Here also is the realm of faith.

So far as possible, interest others in your recreation. This, primarily, because the fight with temptation is a solitary one, and is little helped by games of solitaire. And, secondarily, because leadership in games is a worthy leadership, deserving of any one's ambition.

Not only walk, then, but form a Peripatetic Brotherhood. Not only play tennis, but organize tennis tournaments.

Recreation

Not only study out chess problems, but teach chess to all your neighbors, and have regular chess evenings at your home, with cake and lemonade! In the battle with temptation you need every ally.

I am not urging you to make fun of Satan or make light of temptation. Satan soon proves that he is not to be trifled with, and no one fights temptation long and ever thinks of it shudderless.

No, I do not ask you to make light of temptation, but to make it heavy, to weigh it down with neglect so that it will sink miles deep in the black sea of forgetfulness! Make light of your recreation, or rather, let it make you light, as if it were a life-buoy, floating you to safety and the shore!

For health is happy. Disease, though it rave with insane merriment, is terribly sad. Health is buoyant. Disease is sodden. Purity sparkles. Impurity glowers. Heaven sings. Hell groans eternally.

Do not be deceived by the devil's comic mask. He has a rubber face like a clown's. He can feign mirth almost to perfection. He can flash fire on the waters of Phlegethon till one forgets their blackness of despair.

For every innocent recreation the devil has a counterfeit, a discreation. Look under the surface. Consider results. Going to sport for freedom from temptation, do not let it add to your chains.

Here also, as everywhere else, we need the clear vision of prayer. Let us pray at our play as at our work.

Creator, Thou only Recreator! Holy Spirit, who alone art inspiriting! Christ of the wedding feast, who came that Thy joy might be in us and filled full! Here is a soul outworn with sin, stiffened with the crust of its corruption, depraved with its abandoned tastes, the reality of happiness forgotten in the mad pretence of it. O Christ, I am a leper, my brighter, fairer faculties decayed, eaten away with the corrosion of iniquity. But Thou canst heal lepers; heal even me. From the stumps extend new members. Spread sound flesh over the festering sores. Through the white pall of death irradiate the flush of a healthy pulse. Cause me to run and show myself to the priest, pure, and whole, and happy. Thou who art daily working just such miracles. Thou whose light avails against all darkness, and purity against any corruption. Thou all-attentive, always eager Christ! In Thy beautiful, glad name. Amen.

XVIII

Help from Confession

LL sins are secret sins. All temptations abhor confession. Indeed, the fear of confession is itself the climax of temptation.

We can endure the hidden shame, but not the open shame. Though evermore we must know ourselves as weak and foolish, corrupt and tending to corruption, it seems that it would add a deeper blackness to our degradation if others knew it also.

Yet with this shrinking from confession comes a strange impulsion toward it. "Murder will out." As soon as any sin is committed, a bell begins to ring in the sinner's soul: "Tell it! Tell it! Tell it! Tell!" It is one of the voices of God.

A sin is such a heavy secret to bear alone! If one only had a comrade to lift the little end of it! Temptation is such a terrible battle to fight alone! If one only had a comrade to join the battle-cry, to touch elbows in the march, to whisper behind the barricade!

And always there is an inevitable sense of justice demanding publicity for sin. Because, though the sin was done in the recesses of midnight, its results stare out in the eye of noon. Because there never was a sin, however personal, but injures others. Many others. A constantly radiating multitude of others. Poor reparation, indeed, that they should know who has harmed them; but we feel it their due that we should groan, " It was I. Oh, it was I!"

Doubtless there never was a sinner, though his whole being shrank from the shame of his sin, but longed with agony after confession. A confession that he felt would relieve the terrible, lonely tension. A confession that would begin to set him right with God and man. A confession that he did not dare.

Yet a confession that he knew God wanted. A confession that would prelude forgiveness. For do not the hearts of all sinners ceaselessly moan, " If we confess our sins, He is faithful and just to forgive us our sins, and to cleanse us from all unrighteousness "? Moaning it because they must add, " And I dare not fulfil the condition."

Oh, my brother in temptation and sin, you dare fulfil the condition! It is a difficult condition, but you will not think so.

Confession

For did not the Psalmist truly cry, "Against Thee, Thee only, have I sinned"? He who had sinned so grievously against man. "I acknowledge my transgressions," David cries, " and my sin is ever before *me*. Wash me thoroughly from mine iniquity, and cleanse me from my sin."

"Ah, that is indeed easy," you sigh, relieved. "I am not afraid to confess my sins to God. I confess them continually. Indeed, He knows them already. How could I keep them from Him?"

Brother! if you think it easy to confess your sins to God, you know neither God nor confession.

Saying to God in secret prayer, though you move your lips, though you speak audibly, "God, I have sinned thus and so," is not confession. "Behold, Thou desirest truth in the inward parts," David acknowledges in the same Psalm. It must be a confession of the heart, if it is a confession to God.

What is a heart confession of sin? It is an honest vision of our degradation—and more. It is a terrified recognition of our danger—and more. It is an absolute loathing of our sin—and more. It is an entire admission of defeat.

Is this easy? Have you, with all your prayers, yet attained to it? Does not pride still hold a secret throne in your soul? And does not self-love sit by his side? Do you really hate your sin? Do you honestly even fear it? If you could commit it daily, unseen by God or man and secure against punishment in time or eternity, would you not commit it daily?

Is heart confession easy? Ah, though our prayers say "Miserable sinner," our thoughts add, " I'm not so bad, after all; I'm no worse than others; I mean well; really, it isn't every one that would be conscientious enough to have any inner struggles at all."

Is heart confession easy? Ah, though our prayers say, "Save me, O God," our thoughts add, "Nothing has happened, so far, or very little; I've done enough good to more than balance the rest; it will all come right in the end."

Is heart confession easy? Ah, though our prayers say, "I can do nothing, I am nothing, without Thee, O God," our lives go on in acted independence. Our thoughts say, "I can stop when I really make the effort. I have stopped already many—many times. I will stop for the last time—to-morrow."

Confession

No, no, no! It is easier to stand in the market and proclaim one's sin, in all its detail of shame to proclaim it, easier to write it out and send it to the public press, easier to disclose it to all men everywhere, than truly in one's heart of hearts to abandon it.

And this heart confession must be made to God! Witless and blind is he that calls this easy!

Confess—to God! Have you ever so much as come into God's presence? You will have had no doubt of it. You will have taken off your shoes on that holy ground. You will have covered your eyes against that blinding light. You will have hidden in a cave. You will have fallen at His feet as one dead. You will have said, "Depart from me, for I am a sinful man, O Lord!" or you will have said, "Lord, it is good for me to be here!" or you will have said, "Lord, what wilt Thou have me to do?"

The presence of God! Have you ever stood abashed before an innocent babe, or a pure, sweet maiden, or a mother haloed with divine love? The presence of God is the presence of purity absolute, purity of which the lily is a shadow, and the whitest life ever lived is only its dim reflection.

The presence of God! Has the thunder never appalled you? the down-rush of Niagara, the black energy of a tornado, the crashing devastation of volcano or earthquake? The presence of God is the presence of primal force, the uncomprehended person of all power, from whom at a thought could burst the annihilation of the universe.

The presence of God! Gather into one every form of loveliness upon which your eye has rested, every splendor of majesty, every attribute of genius; concentrate within the compass of your room whatever grandeur you have seen, in the heavens or throughout the varied earth; reach backward to the most distant eons and forward to the limit of time and outward to the bounds of space and draw it all to one focus; magnify and intensify your conception endlessly, by as much as the infinite excels our finite understanding; call this Being before you, and confess your sin!

Will it be easy to confess to God? Will it be easy, standing in that supernal Light, to lay bare your hideousness? Will any pretence of confession avail there? any mask of repentance? any self-delusion of virtue and strength?

This is the real, the basal, confession. No confession before men is more than words, often proud words, often flaunting, shameless words, till confession has thus been made before God.

And after one has thus confessed to God, after he has come to realize what his sin is and what his God is and with a shrinking of great shame has brought the two together, confession before man, any man, all men, is oh, so easy!

As it would be easy, having gazed at the noonday sun, to gaze at a lighted candle; or having lain on the surgeon's table, to endure the sting of a mosquito; or having been on trial before a king, to meet the inquiries of one's neighbor.

As it was with David, who, after his great temptation and deadly fall, wrote his psalm of repentance " For the Chief Musician." " Create in me a clean heart," he cried: " *Then will I teach transgressors Thy ways.*" " Deliver me from bloodguiltiness," he cried: " *And my mouth shall show forth Thy praise.*"

It may not be best to confess to men. Men do not always know our frame, and remember that we are dust. Men do not always remember their own sins, but seek solace from them in remembering the sins of their neighbors. Men can see at the most only a fragment of your character, only the outlines of your temptation. It may be better for the world, and your influence in it, that the world know nothing about your sin.

When a dear one dies, or even a kindly acquaintance, I, for one, avoid looking upon his dead face. He is still alive, and I wish to think of him as alive and not as dead. So let us beware, those of us who have been dead in trespasses and sins and are now alive again in Christ Jesus, lest we needlessly and to no purpose expose the face of our corruption.

But it may be better for the world that we confess our sins before men. Not seldom, by such a confession, a man does more good than by years of apparently flawless living. This is because an example of humility is better than an example of righteousness, and the spectacle of a man being saved is more than the sight of a thousand men that need no saving.

Often, too, the confession of our sins to one man, if not to many men, is an essential of salvation. For his own purposes, God often chooses to save through men. It may not be best for you to receive healing by the secret, direct influence of His Spirit, though in all sincerity you confess your sins in His presence. The Good Physician may have placed His remedies in the hands of some friend.

Confession

Seek, then, the salvation of friendship! There is a man who can bear your sin. Your confession will only bind him more closely to you. He will watch over you. He will show you his own sins. He will help you by letting you help him. He will raise you if you slip back into the ditch. He will question you. The knowledge that he will question you, that you must report to him, that he will know your renewal of sin, will be your mighty safeguard in temptation. He will be to you what Nathan was to David.

It is for you to know whether confession before a man, before all men, is required from you or is best for you and others; rather, it is for you to learn this from God. Of this alone I am sure, that you must confess to God, and that you will know whether you have really confessed to God by this test, that after it confession before men will be easy.

O my God! everything is so easy when I bring Thee into it! Everything is so hard when I leave Thee out of it! Forgetting Thee is to stumble and fall; remembering Thee is to rise again. Forgetting Thee is to go hungry among the swine; remembering Thee is to come to one's self; to say, "I will arise and go to my Father, and will say to Him, 'Father, I have sinned'"; and it is for the Father to run toward us while a great way off, and fall on our neck and kiss us, and with His kisses interrupt our confession. Thou art Majesty, O God; Thou art Power and Justice and terrible Purity; but Thou art also Father. And so, wretched and foul as I am, traitor and rebel as I am, outcast and condemned as I am, I dare to stand before Thee. I do not even fall at Thy feet, for Thou—oh, infinite condescension!—hast fallen upon my neck, with kisses.

XIX

Help from Conscience

YOUR conscience is a disturbance, an annoyance, a condemnation; but is it a help? It shames you, but does it thwart you? Perhaps it checks your fall; but does it draw you upward?

For conscience is more than an alarm bell, arousing the slumbering soul. It is more than a danger signal, warning us from the abyss. It is more than a herald, marching up and down the avenues of the heart, and making proclamation of our sin and disgrace. Conscience is a friend.

A friend, to counsel us. A friend, to whisper comfort and courage. A friend, to take our hand and lead the way. A friend, to talk with in loneliness, and often more blessedly to sit with in silence. Not an enemy, not a tyrant, not a pedagogue, but a friend.

Is our conscience, then, something outside us? No; for does it not speak most loudly when all outside is still? Or, is our conscience our own nature? No, indeed; for often it urgently opposes our own nature. Is it the voice of God speaking to us? No, for we do not pray to our conscience, though conscience often impels us to prayer. What is this mysterious, intangible person or substance?

We should find it less difficult to recognize the triune nature of God if we recognized with more insight the multiform nature of man. Paul saw that he was two Pauls. One delighted in God's law, the other brought his life into captivity to the law of sin and death. The two Pauls warred constantly with each other, and only Christ, who was neither Paul, could give the victory to the right one.

And Paul wrote to the Philippians, "Let this mind be in you, which was also in Christ Jesus"; and to the Corinthians, "We have the mind of Christ."

What is it to have the mind of Christ?

See an inventor put his mind into his machine. In our office is a wonderful steel cylinder, whirling swiftly. A girl sits before it, playing lightly upon a set of keys; and as her fingers touch the well-poised levers the types fall in a shower upon the revolving disk, array themselves in words, erect themselves, and march out in ordered sentences!

Moreover, to take the place of the used types, the machine feeds into itself the columns of last week's paper, lays hold upon each separate type of all the confused myriads, and conducts it through the intricacy of openings to the slot where its comrades lie.

The machine is thinking. It is the solidified idea of its inventor. It is the continuance of his inspiration, his patience, and his skill. The inventor lives somewhere else, but he also veritably lives in our printing room. We have the mind of him.

And this is none the less true because his mind does not always work smoothly. It meets many a clog. One of the falling types will have a bit of wax upon it, and will fall an atom too slowly. One of the marching types will be twisted a trifle in its channel. There will be a crunch of metal, the band will slip, the cylinder will stop, and the girl's fingers play now to no purpose. We have the mind of the inventor, but we have also the mind of sticky types. And the two are at war.

We receive a letter from the inventor, telling us how to manage the machine more perfectly. The other day his representative or agent came in, and showed us much about it. Some day, perhaps, we shall have a visit from the inventor himself, and that will be best of all. Yet continually, day after day in our office, we have the inventor's mind.

And to have the mind of Christ! Of Him without whom was nothing made that was made. Of Him who was in the beginning with God, and was God. Of Him in whom dwells the fulness of God.

To have the mind of Christ! That knows all origins, natures, and destinies. That pierces midnight as if it were daylight and mysteries as if they were axioms. That falters not on any path or before any barrier.

To have the mind of Christ! The mind whose lightest resources are space-wide and time-long. The mind that, owning all things, dares all things. The only mind that never thought defeat.

To have the mind of Christ! The intellect that is all sunshine; of which, indeed, the sunlight is only a reflection. The thought that is serenity and peace.

To have the mind of Christ! That consciousness wherein no foulness ever dwelt. Those breathings of purity, so clear, so sweet. That infinite sea of uncontaminated thought.

Is it possible? Nay; can it be other than this? Has the Allwise Inventor left no mind in His creation? No prolongation and witness of Himself? Then He would be less than the inventors He has made.

No; in every loathing of the wrong and impulse toward the right, in every sorrow for sin and shame at a fall, in every debate before temptation, and even in the quiet, monotonous, untempted doing of good, I recognize the mind of Christ left with me when He made me. It is the Original Virtue, combating the Original Sin!

Impeded, denied, disowned? Yes, how many times! The types of my life go astray. They fall crooked, they run awry, they break and clog and ruin. None the less for all that, precisely the more for all that if it results victorious, I have the mind of Christ!

My conscience, then, is that whereby I know with—*scio cum*—God. It warns, but only when God would warn. It condemns, but only when God would condemn. It can also approve and advise, comfort and cheer. It is a friend, being a representative of the friendly God.

Shall I forget my origin? Aloft, in the counsels of the Most High, my nature was devised, my name first called! From infinite reaches of spirit and power the Maker drew my substance and my form. Lovingly He thought it all out, how I—not generic Man, but I, this sole I—should look and act and feel and think. Patiently, through eons of the past, He planned—for me. Masterfully, through ranges of omnipotencies, He searched for my component parts and fashioned them in one. And in their midst He set—His mind.

Oh, the wonder of it, the joy of it, the glory of it! What treasure have I, to match my conscience? Dearer than the apple of my eye, for it is the eye of God. Dearer than the power of thought, for it is the mind of Christ. Strip me of all things else, blind me, divest me of all other apprehension, all stores of memory and knowledge, and leave me with this sole possession, and I shall be infinitely rich!

So I will exult in my conscience. I will fear only its silence. When it upbraids me, I will be only the more sure that I have the mind of Christ. When it warns me, I will hold up my head, for the mind of Christ has spoken, and from my very soul.

So I will cherish my conscience, and I will magnify it. Yes, I will foster and enlarge the mind of Christ within me!

For we must forget our comparison. Man is no machine. Still less has the Inventor gone away and left him to himself. He is invisible. He has written the Letter. He has sent the Representative. But He is also here. And both Letter and Representative assure us that He is here.

And man is more than matter, inert and passive. This machine can remake itself, can enlarge or contract its dimensions, can thrust from it the mind of its Inventor, or enlarge its chambers, reach forth, and draw more of that mind to itself.

I have a mind for books, a mind whereby I revel in history and biography, in essays and poems, a mind that can store up facts and follow reasoning. There is nothing I can do with this mind that I cannot do with my conscience, the mind of Christ within me.

My book mind—I can stifle or inspire, neglect or train, dwarf or develop. I can feed it with Voltaire or Isaiah, with Tupper or Shakespeare. I can use it or tie it up. I can enrich it with the spoils of all centuries, or I can let it go squalid and bare.

So with my conscience, the mind of Christ within me. I can send it to school; for as Christ was born a babe in Bethlehem, so His mind is born undeveloped in our souls. That school is the

Bible, and the example and words of good men, and prayer and honest meditation.

I can exercise my conscience, setting it to hard tasks, overcoming desires and tendencies and temptations. I can feed it and use it and develop it into massive strength, and ever as it grows I can make more room for it in my life.

Or—and how easily!—I can lull my conscience to sleep; kick it, all stupid, into a corner; push it back when it rises, and bid it be quiet. I can afford it no teaching, no training, no models. I can cramp its quarters and stint its food. I can do all this, and more. I can kill my conscience.

Kill the mind of Christ within me! Slay the memorial of Himself which the Maker left with His creation! Destroy that whereby I think with God!

So that henceforth I am like a telescope whose great lens is broken, and the heavens are empty to it.

Forbid it, O my Father! Forbid it, loving Redeemer! Forbid it, Thou Comforter divine! That would be the axe upon the stretched cable. That would be the final sin, unpardonable, because it could no longer desire pardon. Forgive me, that I have so often made a mock of conscience.

Conscience

Forgive me, that I have so often followed the mind of flesh and scorned the mind of Christ, or in my folly tried to follow both! I will no longer forget my upper self, that destiny which Thou hadst for me before the world was. Henceforth my priceless treasure shall be this link that binds me to it, this mysterious token of Thy purpose for me. Evermore now I will strive to think with Thee more perfectly, till I in Thee and Thou in me are made perfect in one, and my conscience has become Thy conscience! The thought were blasphemy, Lord Jesus, hadst Thou not made it Thy prayer for me. In Thy strength I seek it, through Thy grace I await it. Amen.

XX

Help from Friendship

THE temptations that assail one in solitude are best to be met in a crowd, but the temptations of the crowd are never best met in solitude. There is no temptation that a friend cannot help us defeat.

A man who falls under many temptations may have many acquaintances but he cannot have many friends.

Because a friend is some one who holds you to your best self, while an acquaintance accepts you, or leaves you, as you choose to be. An acquaintance studies to make himself pleasing to you, but a friend studies to make you pleasing to God.

An acquaintance dares not or cares not to offend you. A friend does not dare *not* to offend you, if your displeasure is the road to your reformation.

And so a foolish man is most often known by this, that he drives away his friends and cleaves to his acquaintances, who will not cleave to him. Thus he cherishes his complacency, and his sins.

Friendship 175

My brother! If you are tempted, and have a friend, count him chief of your worldly goods. Cling to his side, though his dagger pierce you daily. It is a surgeon's lancet.

And if you have no friend, while ten thousand men and women nod to you and greet you in parlors, seek a friend as your most earnest worldly pursuit, and beg a friend in your prayers to heaven.

How few friends there are!

How few take time for friendship! We have long hours for gold and silver and banknotes or for what we boastfully call our work in the world, and we have grudged minutes for the gold of eternity which is character and the work of eternity which is fashioning it. Review yesterday. Did it hold, gathering all the minutes, half an hour for friendship?

Yet friendship requires time. All good things need time, and the best things the most time. You cannot in chance encounters and hasty glimpses grow at home in another life, and learn the temptations that the other himself after a lifetime with himself neither understands nor conquers. Elisha, in that dark chamber of the Shunammite, stretched himself upon the boy, once and again, his mouth upon his mouth, his eyes upon his eyes, his hands upon his hands, before the flesh waxed warm and the child opened his eyes. Thus Elisha acted a parable of friendship.

And how few take pains for friendship! How few plan for it! It is treated as a haphazard, fortuitous thing. May good luck send us friends; we will not go after them. May favoring fortune bind our friendships; we will take no stitches ourselves. Review yesterday, and all your yesterdays. Did they open with any thought for friendship—its pursuit, its retention, its glorification?

Yet friendship requires painstaking. No art is so difficult, no craft so arduous. Roll a ball of clay and expect it to become a rose in your hand, but never expect acquaintanceship, without care and thought, to blossom into friendship.

Trade is not conducted without a programme and much toil. Legislation is not obtained by aimless talk. No device or employment or phase of society cares for itself. But friendship is the most intricate of trades, the loftiest of laws, the climax of society; and shall it care for itself?

How few have insight for friendship! You must know more than the color of your friend's eyes,—the very hue of his fancies; more than his height,—the reachings of his aspirations; and more than his weight,—the unseen burdens that depress his soul.

How few have sympathy for friendship! It is easy to say, "I am so sorry for you," but does your heart ache while you say it? It is easy to say, "I congratulate you," but does all the sky shine brighter for your friend's joy? Is his food meat to you? Does blood really flow through the nexus of your lives?

And how few have courage for friendship! The daring that offers blame instead of the desired praise. The boldness that lays a healing finger upon the hurt. The faithfulness that adheres to faultfinding when one longs for occasion to commend. The loving strength that will even sacrifice friendship rather than be untrue to it.

For friendship is based on independence. If I am your friend, you are more necessary to me than your friendship. If I can know you pure and wise and beautiful, I can dispense with your friendship. Or rather, I can intermit it, knowing well how eternity will restore it. This is the high, sad test of friendship. Fortunate are you if you know a man who can stand the test. Alas for you if you ever require it!

This being friendship, how helpful it is in temptation! Friendship takes you out of yourself in alluring requirement, and the sinful man longs to get away from himself. Friendship gives you a new self, the self of your friend; and a new life, the life of your friend; and the sinful man longs immeasurably for a new self, a new life.

For there is no other way to win friends than this, that you be a friend.

That *is* why friendship is helpful—not so much because it helps you as because it compels you to help your friend. Selfishness is the foundation of sin, and friendship is the destruction of selfishness.

If you would find your arms around a man, extend your hands to lift him up. You are in a pit yourself, but you can always find some one in a lower pit.

Go out after friendship. As a man prospects for golden nuggets, seek the soul you can help, though ever so little. As you wash the sands for that, you will be washing the stains from your soul.

Go out after friendship. It is well to company with the wise, the pure, the beautiful. They too need friends.

They have become wise and pure and beautiful because, in part, they have entered into the sageness and health and grace of friendship. They need to continue it by helping you, entering into friendship with you. It is half of friendship, a blessed half, to receive where you cannot yet give.

But you can also give. No life so wretched, no soul so debauched, but it has something to bestow. Though only a look of love, only a word of kindliness—*only!* when those are king's treasures! Indeed, O my brother despairing amid your temptations, if I were to say that you had nothing you could give another man, of guidance, inspiration, or grace, you would be prompt to deny me.

Give it! Give it! Pour yourself out, your best self, for some one. Only by serving the one has a man ever come to serve humanity.

Give it! Give it! In original fashion, your own fashion, though no one in all the world has yet done just that thing for another. Or, though it is a very commonplace thing that any one might be doing for another.

Give it! Give it! Whether the object of your friendship becomes a friend or not. It is a most hindering error to suppose that two are required for a friendship. The most enriching friendships of all time have been lonely ones. Be *you* a friend.

Give it! Give it! Through ridicule, scorn, rebuff; through failure and fainting and fear; through doubt and despair. Friendship has no yesterdays and no to-morrows.

And as you give it—however little—to one who has less, you will want to give more; and as you give more, you will want to give your best, and a great, pure longing for the best will spring up within you,—for the best, that you may give. It is the running channel that enlarges itself.

Yes, and it is the running channel that is clean. As the currents of love and helpfulness begin to flow, how they will loosen that encrusted vice, how they will wash away that foulness, and how, as they grow in bulk and power, they will sweep the filth from your soul!

Is friendship, then, to be our saviour from sin? Do we need no Cross? Do we need no Christ?

Ah, there is no friendship without the Friend! Neither can it be begun, nor continued, nor enjoyed, without the Friend. I have said that friendship does not require two; it does, but the other is Christ!

His life was an incarnation of friendship. The angels sung it over the manger, "Good will to men." The lepers knew it, upon whom He laid unfearing hands. The outcasts knew it, with whom He sat at meat. Doubters knew it, whom He led with gentle patience. His enemies knew it, whom His love condemned. His disciples knew it, whom with His dying breath He called friends. The great world shall yet know it, being drawn to the lifted cross of friendship.

That the Almighty is our Friend. That the universe, all universes, time and space and all providence, are friendly. That we should be friends. That the way of friendship is the way of the Cross. This is the message of Christ.

He sought out the lowest. He needed no answering friendship; though He longed for it, and longs for it. He gave His best, His all. He gave unstintedly, whatever men would take. He gave humbly, with no parade, more lavishly by Sychar's well than in Pilate's hall. He gave persistently, unchecked by ridicule, undismayed by ingratitude, undaunted by hostility.

He had no sins for His friendship to wash away. The channel of His life was unimpeded, and the fulness of God swept through it. But His friendship is the living water that washes away our sins.

Friend, Friend, endlessly my Friend! From the beginning of beginnings my Friend! Through all everlastings my Friend! Amid all sins and temptations, all failures and shame, my Friend and only my Friend! My cleansing and purity, O Friend! My confidence and upholding, O Friend! My hope and joy, O Friend! Implanter of love and grace, my Friend! Inspirer of sympathy and patience, my Friend! Giver of insight and wisdom, my Friend! When others fall away in sorrowing despair of me, when I abandon myself and lie down in the dust, when my world is my sinful desire, still, still my Friend! Into new courage and the upleaping of will, into the glad dawn of purity and manhood, into the strife that means victory at last, Thy friendship, O my Friend! With no postponing, with no reserve, with no doubt, now, now, all that I am, all that Thou art, I a friend and Thou my Friend, to-day, all days, forever and ever. Amen.

www.ingramcontent.com/pod-product-compliance
Lightning Source LLC
Chambersburg PA
CBHW031352040426
42444CB00005B/261